Work Like a Woman

Also by Mary Portas

HOW TO SHOP
SHOP GIRL

For more information on Mary Portas and her books,
see her website at www.maryportas.com

Mary Portas
Work Like a Woman

A manifesto for change

WITH MEGAN LLOYD DAVIES

Printed and bound in Great Britain by Clays Ltd, Elcograf S.p.A.

Penguin Random House is committed to a sustainable future for our business, our readers and our planet. This book is made from Forest Stewardship Council® certified paper.

BLACK SWAN

TRANSWORLD PUBLISHERS
61–63 Uxbridge Road, London W5 5SA
www.penguin.co.uk

Transworld is part of the Penguin Random House group of companies
whose addresses can be found at global.penguinrandomhouse.com

First published in Great Britain in 2018 by Bantam Press
an imprint of Transworld Publishers
Black Swan edition published 2019

A CIP catalogue record for this book
is available from the British Library.

ISBN
9781784163624

Typese
Pri

f

CONTENTS

PREFACE

*Here's to strong women: may we know them,
may we be them, may we raise them.*

The subject of women and the culture we work in exploded into the public consciousness as I was writing this book. Sexual harassment, the gender pay gap: skeletons have come tumbling out of the closet during 2017 and 2018.

It's clear that work is working against women, even the most successful.

It's not outright discrimination any more. (Usually.) In fact, we've got enough of a stake in the workforce today for many of us to believe that women are doing okay. We're given jobs, earn about the same as men, until we have children, and some of us get to the top.

But the subtle barriers facing us range from our often doing jobs that are financially undervalued, to workplaces that don't truly accommodate our roles as carers, or a ceiling that is all too often not made of glass but concrete.

And fifty years after we entered the paid workforce in large numbers, we are finally beginning to feel less grateful about the progress we've made – and are starting to get angrier about how much further we have to go before we achieve parity with men.

I welcome this. We need to be angry.

We are as strong, capable and talented as men, and need to start pushing for a faster pace of change to allow us to realize our true potential. Who knows where that will take us individually?

But this issue is about more than each one of us. It's about something far bigger collectively. It's about power. And the leaders who make the decisions that intimately affect our day-to-day lives.

Where power once lay in the hands of kings and bishops, today it's with the leaders of politics, business, technology and finance. These are the people whose decisions dictate whose pocket will be worse hit by budget cuts, the pensions and prospects of millions of workers, and which war we will fight in.

And women aren't making these decisions because we aren't at the top in anything like equal numbers to men.

Just two out of sixty-one British prime ministers have been women. There's never been a female governor of the Bank of England since it was set up in 1694. Just one of the nine members of its current committee is a woman. A mere six of our 100 biggest companies are headed by a woman.

This top-line data alone tells us we haven't got a foothold in the door of power. It's more a toe over the threshold.

It means we're working – and living – in a system that doesn't reflect the things we often want, or our priorities.

Meanwhile self-serving competition, arrogance and focus on individual wins over the collective good are sadly too prevalent in the behaviour of many of our leaders today. This is why we have to make work more equal, allowing women to rise and take their equal place at the top of power struc-tures. Creating a better balance between men and women will help us to start to shape a future that truly reflects all our needs, thoughts and considerations together.

Instead of suppressing women's talents, values and expertise, putting essentially feminine qualities like empathy, collaboration and flexibility, strength, courage and resilience at the heart of the system will create a radical shift in how we work – and live.

That's not to say all women and men necessarily have – or don't have – these qualities. Each one of us embodies a million different aspects of the complicated kaleidoscope that is personality. But, like it or not, certain qualities have traditionally been pigeonholed as 'masculine' and 'feminine' so that's my starting point.

And I believe all of us would benefit from seeing more of what's considered feminine valued at work because women may be at the sharper end of this, but many men are affected too.

Simply tweaking how things stand with a leadership scheme here or a pay rise there will not create the kind of change we need. Neither will paying public lip service while keeping a tight private grip on the status quo.

There must be a radical re-evaluation of how we work – and a cultural shift at the heart of it.

That's why we've got to work together.

Work is central to all our lives but only half of us are making the most of it – and we're all losing out because of that. It's time to find a new way to work that will help us create a better future for all of us – and our children.

It is time for change.

1

Is Work Working Against Us?

*'The secret of change is to focus all of your energy,
not on fighting the old, but on building the new.'*
Socrates

I'm sitting in the Arco Café in Knightsbridge and don't know which is more overpowering: the smell of fat or the reek of fag smoke.

It's 1981; I'm twenty-one and work as a window dresser at Harrods.

'I can't believe Elaine didn't get the job,' Fiona says. 'We've got to do something.'

Fiona, who works with me on the back windows, is outraged. Our colleagues Elaine and Roger both went for a promotion and he got it. They're equally talented but we thought Elaine would get the job because she's been at Harrods far longer than Roger and that's usually how things work.

'We've got to go on strike or something,' Fiona hisses. 'Demonstrate. Contact our union.'

I stare at her. The only women I know who demonstrate are the ones at Greenham Common Women's Peace Camp, who chain themselves to fences in protest against nuclear arms. It doesn't look very comfortable.

'Don't you see, Mary?' Fiona says, with a withering look. 'If we don't do something then none of us stand a chance. The men will always get the jobs.'

I don't really think too much about this kind of stuff. Isn't that just how things are? The only woman I've known who was in charge of something was my head teacher. And that's because it was a convent school run by nuns.

We all knew who ruled the roost at home when I was growing up: my mother, Theresa. She looked after me, my sister, brothers and dad. No car, part-time evening work as a cleaner, cooking, washing and cleaning for six and still Dad's dinner was on the table the moment he got through the door. She was never not working.

But Dad was the one who came home from work clutching the staff newspaper with his photo on the front page. Dad was the person who put money on the collection plate when we went to St Helen's every Sunday.

In the eyes of the outside world, he was the one in charge.

But as I sit in the café with Fiona, I think of my brothers – Michael, Joe and Lawrence – and realize how unfair it would be if my sister Tish or I missed out on a job in favour of one of them just because they're men.

And then I think about Elaine. It's true what Fiona is saying. There are a lot of men in charge at Harrods: in fact, it's all men who run the display department where we work.

Berge is head of front windows, Keith looks after side while Peter heads home and interior display. Then there is David, head of ground-floor display, Andrew on the first floor, Alan on the second, Antonio on the third and Paul on the fourth. Lou is the deputy display manager (his name isn't short for Louise) and above us all is the big boss, John.

(To be fair, there *is* a woman in the management offices: a secretary called Jane.)

Fiona is right. Floor after floor of men are managing women, who rarely get the chance to manage them back. Elaine has been sidelined just because she's a woman.

And that is so not on.

'What are we going to do?' I say.

Within days, a few of us are stamping up and down the pavement outside Harrods' windows but we aren't exactly a force to be reckoned with. Most of our women colleagues don't want to stick their head above the parapet, however much they agree with us. We try to mobilize the union but soon realize that our protestations are falling on deaf ears. Not long after, we melt into the background again.

Soon, Fiona will leave Harrods and in time I will also resign to start a freelance career in window display. Because although I'm not sure where I want to go, I know one thing after my first glimpse of sex discrimination in the workplace: I want to create opportunities that, back then as a woman, Harrods will never give me.

If you're aged forty or above, this story might seem familiar. The world of work was a very different place even as recently as twenty years ago – and men were largely in charge. But if you're younger, maybe you're wondering what it's got to do with you. There are lots of women managers in your office, after all.

Humour me. Read on. Be we Baby Boomers, Generation Xers or Millennials, I'm afraid we're all in this together, because the world we work in is often working against us.

Take retail, my area of expertise: 60 per cent of its employees are women, and women also make or influence 85 per cent of all purchasing decisions. That means we're usually responsible for buying everything from our old man's pants to big-ticket items like holidays. Retail is a world that women drive both financially and practically. And yet, we've only got 10 per cent of the positions on retail executive boards.

That's kind of perverse, isn't it? A business made up of women, sustained by women, but hardly any of us make it to the top?

It's the same in many industries. We know about the male domination of politics, banking and engineering. But they're also at the top of industries that, like retail, are very female-dominated. Teaching, say, or medicine.

Even in hairdressing – and if that isn't a female-driven industry then I don't know what is – all the famous names are male: from Vidal Sassoon, Trevor Sorbie and Toni & Guy through to John Frieda, Nicky Clarke and Sam McKnight. But can you name a single famous female hair stylist?

Thought not.

The reality is that most industries have more women at the bottom and more men at the top.

So why is this? Do women lack stamina? Or ambition? Are we too difficult to work with? Or are we just really average at our jobs?

Some people say we lack ambition, that women don't reach for the top because we get so far and then life, family and work clash too often for many of us to devote the attention to a career that success demands.

(You know the kind of people who say that: it's usually the ones with someone at home doing everything from childcare to picking up the dry cleaning so there's nothing else for them to worry about except working eighty hours a week.)

Then there are those who believe the way women work means we're not equipped to rise to the top. We might be too passive, unambitious or focused on children. You know the kind of thing.

Yeah, yeah. Enough of the excuses.

There is a reason why women don't get to the top in the same numbers as men and it has zero to do with our shortcomings. Systemic barriers are what stop us.

Systemic barriers at work affect the whole culture and everyone working within it – particularly women. Why? Because they're part of a working code that was created by men for men.

Even more specifically: a code created by men who were powerful in terms of their class and ethnicity, as well as their gender: white, wealthy alpha males, to be exact.

They're the people who have pretty much had a monopoly on getting to the top for a very long time – and the way we work today is still rooted in the alpha culture they created long ago.

If you want to succeed, you need to fit the mould. So alpha men do well and so do some alpha women, myself included. For a start I'm white, and, although I came from a working-class background, I had enough talent and drive – and a few lucky breaks – to get to the top.

But I am more of an exception than the rule, and until we adapt our working culture, shifting its focus and values to reflect a more modern world and diverse society, we will still often funnel only one particular type of person to the top.

And, sadly, it ain't usually a woman.

The effect of these systemic barriers is that although women certainly start off strong in the workplace (let's not forget that we've already outperformed boys at school and are 35 per cent more likely than them to go to university), we end up lagging behind in our careers.

We earn less: 81p for every £1 that a man makes. We're also promoted less in our paid work and do far more of the junior-level jobs than the senior ones – making up nearly three-quarters of the entry workforce and holding just 32 per cent of director-level posts.

Not exactly uplifting reading, is it?

But the world of work is like this because most businesses still have an alpha working culture. And it's a culture that respects and over-rewards so-called 'masculine' qualities, like risk-taking, competition and single-minded, myopic focus. Meanwhile, more 'feminine' traits like collaboration, resilience, empathy and compassion are consistently devalued.

Alpha culture views most emotions with suspicion. Logic is king! Instinct: what's that? It's also heavily invested in dominance and the drive to 'win' – which often creates an office environment where people are pitting their skills against each other to compete for money or seniority.

Linear advancement up the ladder is prioritized over collaboration; single-minded focus is encouraged to the detriment of any life outside work – including family. Extreme risk-taking to prove 'strength', and the inability to show 'weakness' by admitting mistakes, become the norm.

We can all see the effect this is having. Look at the world around us. And, yet, nothing is really changing.

Of course lots of us – men and women – are ambitious, risk-taking and competitive. And not everyone, and every business, works like this. But to some degree, these dynamics are at play in every sphere of work. And they are driven by our alpha working culture. It means work often ends up resembling a battleground as we compete against each other, build strategic alliances and carefully keep track of the balance of power.

Put all this together – the structure of the way we work and the qualities that are rewarded – and most women, at best, are held back. At worst, we are excluded from the top.

But, as important as the issue of women leaders is, this isn't just about those who want to aim high and are stopped in their tracks by a way of working that doesn't work for them. It affects us all because the jobs we typically do are not as financially valued as those often done by men.

Take a look at the thirty lowest-paid jobs in the US. Women are far more likely to do twenty-three of them, including food server, housekeeper and childcare worker. Meanwhile men are far more likely to do twenty-six of the thirty highest-paying jobs, including chief executive, architect and computer engineer.

Now, architects and computer engineers are important. But why are men mostly doing these jobs? And why aren't vocational, caring jobs considered important, too, and paid better?

Even when we try to do better-paid jobs traditionally done by men, we're stymied.

US researchers, who looked at fifty years of census data from 1950 to 2000, found that wages fell by 57 per cent when women took over jobs in summer camps and parks that had previously been done by men. When they became biologists, the wages dropped by 18 per cent.

What happened, though, when men took over jobs that, traditionally, women had done?

You've got it. The pay went up.

In the 1940s, computer programming was considered 'women's work' – a nice bit of typing code that was an exciting alternative to being a secretary. (Tell that to Rear Admiral Grace Hopper – one of the pioneers of programming.) And there we leave them for a few decades, quietly getting on with the job.

In the 1980s tech became the money-making future. Men moved into the industry and programming suddenly got way more complex. Supposedly. The nerd was born, recruitment started to favour men and pay increased. Today women hold just one in four jobs in the industry.

Even in occupations dominated by women, men earn more. The education workforce is two-thirds female but in the UK male teachers earn on average £2 more per hour than women.

How on earth is all this still happening?

And if what you've read so far doesn't make you thump the table with rage, I suggest you put down this book and check yourself for a pulse.

So how did we end up here? It's simple, really: men were in charge of the formal workplace – and the way it works – for a very long time.

Women didn't enter formal employment *en masse* until about fifty years ago, and today we're almost half of the workforce. More than 70 per cent of UK women aged sixteen to sixty-four work. It's a trend seen everywhere from Japan and Germany to the US.

But we're stuck in a Catch-22: we can't get to the top because of the codes created by men, and we can't change things if we don't get to the top.

Some people think quotas are an answer to this – that things would improve if women were given half of all corporate board seats tomorrow – but I don't think anything will really change until we question the culture of the way we work.

Alpha culture's masterstroke has been to make it seem so 'normal' that, even as the demographics of the workplace have changed so radically, we haven't questioned it. Isn't this just how things are?

No.

It's about our values, the things we attach importance to, and our behaviours. And this is expressed in even the most seemingly insignificant of ways.

Fashion – my industry – is a brilliant case in point.

The BBC is a national, publicly funded broadcaster, which represents a nation pretty evenly split between men and women. But amid all the airtime and correspondents it devotes to football, and the Premier League in particular, there is no one dedicated to talking about fashion.

Football certainly has a huge social significance. But even though the fashion industry was worth almost ten times what the Premier League was to the UK economy in 2014, it obviously isn't considered important by those divvying up the budgets at the BBC.

Go figure.

It's the same in business: certain focuses, behaviours and characteristics tell us a lot about the values held by organizations. They tell us that we're still working along traditional masculine alpha lines.

I should know. I did it myself for years.

Until I couldn't do it any more.

2

Can We Be Part of the Tribe?

'Know the rules so you can break them effectively.'
Dalai Lama

I'm tempted to take off my whole outfit and start again as I stand in front of the mirror, dithering. Do the flowery trousers work? Are the rings too much? Do I need to tone the whole thing down?

I really need to decide because I'm running late.

It could be 1978 all over again.

But I'm not a teenager about to go on a night out.

I am a fifty-something mother-of-three who has run her own business for years, and is now often asked to give business talks because I'm an expert on the retail sector.

I'm doing one today at a conference and will go on stage after Liam Fox MP. He's sure to be wearing a grey suit and most of the audience will be too. Grey suits are the accepted uniform of working men in positions of power. The most daring it gets is a purple stripe in a tie, perhaps a flash of a coloured sock.

So what I'm wondering is this: what will they make of me when I appear on the podium in floral trousers and a cobalt-blue jacket? Will I fit into the tribe?

Then I find I don't care.

It's taken me a long time not to care, to come to understand who I am and feel confident enough to look the way I do. I leave the house knowing that what I'm wearing is a reflection of me: colourful, confident and slightly flamboyant. This is my kind of outfit and I'm good at what I do and sure of what I'm talking about. I don't need a suit to impress people or feel part of their tribe.

But we all grapple with questions like these almost every day. Humans are tribal. Even if we're not a complete fit for the group we're part of, we like to create social groups whose rules we understand and can work to.

So, to start understanding the alpha tribe a little better (and we have to understand it in order to unpick it), we must look at it in its purest form: almost exclusively male institutions.

Let's start by rewinding a couple of decades back to when Caitlin Zaloom, an American anthropologist, decided to study the very male world of financial trading floors in London and Chicago.

What she found was a stringent pecking order, men rising up the ranks, thanks to extreme financial risk-taking and such excessive shows of bravado that two paramedics were needed on standby at the Chicago Board of Trade in case physical fights broke out.

No. You didn't read that wrong.

God knows if the paramedics are still there today. But I see little change from that kind of competitive behaviour in the way that industry and others still work, and perhaps that's reflected in the fact that women still make up only 15 per cent of the financial trading workforce.

Similarly, when MPs examined what was holding women back in the intelligence services, they identified an immovable layer of middle management with a traditional male mindset. They also saw an alpha-male management culture that rewarded those who were loud or aggressive in pursuing their career, leaving others behind.

But alpha culture is not always found in the most obvious places. It can hide itself well too. TV production or tech offices might be full of free-thinking creatives who enjoy the onsite yoga studio and napping pods, but don't mistake a progressive top layer for real change.

Just ask Apple.

In 2017, the company unveiled its new California 'campus', for 12,000 employees, which had taken eight years to build. It was so carefully thought out that even the stone covering the gym walls in the 100,000-foot fitness and wellness centre was 'from just the right quarry in Kansas, and has been carefully distressed, like a pair of jeans'.

Fabulous attention to detail, Apple. Imagine how long it took to dream up that one.

Strange, then, that no one managed to think about putting any childcare facilities on site. The combined minds of 250 architects and countless Apple bosses didn't think to build any.

And what they implicitly communicated to their employees by focusing so heavily on design and gym facilities was that beauty – be it the building's or the staff's – was important. The ability of their employees to integrate their working lives with those minor, messy responsibilities called children was not.

But let's be clear here: women don't get a free pass on all this. Alpha culture might have been put in place by men, but we're also working alongside them and, in many cases, perpetuating the status quo.

Now if there weren't many women working, I might be able to understand why the culture of how we work hasn't really changed over the past few decades. If, say, there were just a few of us in the workforce and the rest of us were sitting around posting pictures of cushion covers on our Pinterest boards I could maybe grasp why adapting our working culture to better reflect and reward women's strengths might not be considered a priority.

But we're half the workforce and only a third of its managers, directors and senior officials. That's rubbish by anyone's standards.

The workplace is still working against us and, as much as I respect Sheryl Sandberg, who argues that women need to adapt their behaviour to better suit the status quo, I'm more of a Gloria Steinem fan. 'It's not about integrating into a not-so-good system,' she has said. 'It's about transforming it and making it better. If women have to acquire all the characteristics of a corporate world, it's probably not worth it.'

Too right, Gloria. I don't want to lean into a system that is entrenched in a working world that's quite frankly dated, limited and controlling.

It's bloody well time it changed.

Until women have true equality in the workplace across every discipline and pay scale, we will never be able to influence the way in which we, and future generations, work and live.

But that's not to say men have got all this sewn up. Women bear the brunt of the shortcomings of how we work today but many men are disadvantaged too. Some are forced into choosing work as a priority over family in order to be seen as promotion material. Others are as hemmed in as many women by having to ape alpha behaviour that is not an easy fit for them. And most of the men who are doing well out of the status quo are perpetuating it because that's what they've been taught to do. Just as women can accept their lot and believe this is just the way it is and always will be.

But it has to change if women are to have any chance of truly staking their claim in the world of work – and improving things for us all.

Inspirational and innovative change can be found in the most unexpected places. The world of offshore oil drilling is macho, tough and risky. But something fascinating happened when bosses at two rigs in the Gulf of Mexico decided to change how they worked.

The workforce on the rigs was 90 per cent male and they lived together offshore for two weeks at a time, doing twelve-hour shifts and on call twenty-four hours a day.

Bosses wanted to improve workplace safety and performance and, to do this, decided to shift the focus from individual performance to long-term goals. In essence, they wanted to change the culture of the rigs from having colleagues competing against each other to working together.

Changes were introduced to make that happen. Workers were asked to shut down the platform at first sight of a potentially dangerous situation – with no blame attached if they misjudged it, even though shutdowns were expensive. They were also encouraged to intervene when colleagues breached safety rules. By sharing information instead of hiding mistakes, they started to be open about them and to analyse them as a way to learn. Finally, the men stopped hiding their emotions – and the toll of their job on their family lives in particular – and started to talk about how they felt.

Slowly but surely the culture on the rigs changed. The 'biggest, baddest roughnecks' stopped rising to the top. Instead the men who cared about their fellow workers, were good listeners, and were willing to learn did. The link between macho behaviour and good performance was broken. The accident rate fell by 84 per cent. Productivity, efficiency and reliability improved.

The world of symphony orchestras couldn't be more different from that of oil rigs. But it was also traditionally male-dominated because, although contenders auditioned, they were usually male students hand-picked by teachers.

Then, in 1952, the Boston Symphony Orchestra decided to find out if there was a way to recruit more women, and started doing 'blind' auditions by asking musicians to play behind a screen to hide their identity. Other orchestras followed suit in the subsequent decades and some, in addition to screens, also placed thick carpet on the audition stage so that lighter footsteps didn't give away the gender of the auditionee. Today more than half of the players in the top 250 US orchestras are women.

Now, an oil rig and an orchestra are specific working environments. It's not exactly stacking supermarket shelves or running a team of sales people. But, however exotic, these examples show that the way to create a new work environment and a better business model is to think carefully about what you want to change – the working culture, the demographic of the staff – and find ways to make that happen.

They prove that, by implementing new ideas, alpha working culture can change. Radically. And they show that men – as well as women – can benefit from that change.

3

One of the Boys

'I believe the old boys' network is a powerful one. No one gives up power and privilege willingly, do they?'
Quentin Bryce, politician

My mate Russ has been driving me all over London on the back of his motorbike today. Time is tight because I'm seeing ten major retailers about a new project I'm working on. I've got fifteen minutes with each of them to convince them to buy into it.

It's 2011 and I'm making a TV show for Channel 4 called *Mary's Bottom Line*. In it, I've partnered up with the lingerie manufacturer Headen & Quarmby to create Kinky Knickers, a line of British-made lingerie.

I've been presenting TV shows for a few years now, going into struggling retail businesses and using my expertise to help the owners, who've rarely had access to the skills you learn in bigger companies and have often lost their way.

I love making change happen for people and have quickly realized that this particular programme is about more than underwear. It's about a town, a community and people severely affected by job losses. Headen & Quarmby has had a factory in Middleton, near Manchester, since 1935. In its heyday, sixty machinists worked there. But then, like so many others, the company was forced to send production abroad in the drive for cheaper prices.

The programme is looking at whether it's possible to breathe new life back into British manufacturing. Can we make something that not only provides jobs but also competes with cheap foreign imports?

Turning up on my first day, I saw the impact that local unemployment had had as scores of young people queued for the machinist jobs we were looking to fill at the factory. Many of them had never worked and were desperate to do so.

But while I know how to brand, market and sell, I had no idea how to make knickers. We needed someone with the skills to teach these new young recruits about the job they were there to do. I found wonderful Myra, an expert seamstress who had lost her job when the factory she worked in closed, stacking shelves in Tesco. Although she agreed to help us, Myra could only spare us the evenings. She wasn't going to give up a secure job for a project she didn't think could work, given what she'd seen happen to her industry. We started shooting the programme at night as Myra trained the machinists.

Now I'm in London to secure large, regular orders to keep Kinky Knickers financially afloat. Success is dependent on selling at volume, and the day has gone well so far. Boots, Liberty, ASOS, Selfridges, Harvey Nichols and House of Fraser will all place orders.

I'm on a roll and the adrenalin is pumping as I walk into the head offices of another major retailer. Peter Cross, the then managing partner at my retail consultancy agency, has come to meet me to help land this high-street giant.

As we walk to the chief executive's office, portraits of

former CEOs – one man after another – stare down at us from the walls.

'Good afternoon,' the chief exec says, as we sit down with him. He looks at Peter's wrist. 'A Panerai,' he says. 'Such a great watch.'

He might as well have unzipped his pants to see whose was bigger. Try as I might to enter the discussion, the male chief executive's focus stays fixed on Peter.

'So what is your wholesale price? What margins are you hoping for?'

Question after question is directed at Peter, who grows increasingly embarrassed and uncomfortable.

'This is a very personal project for Mary,' he says, as he tries to drag me into the conversation. 'She created the concept, designed the range and pulled a factory team together to produce it.'

'Great,' the chief executive replies, his eyes darting sideways at me before swivelling back to Peter. 'So what's your proposed sell-through?'

By about minute eight, I'm ready to shove a pair of Kinky Knickers down his throat. The moment our time is up, I stand up to leave. The chief executive looks at me, seemingly surprised that I am leaving rather than being dismissed.

We don't get the order.

Now, if I had challenged this man and asked him why everything – from the questions he asked to the eye contact he gave – was directed at my male colleague I'm sure he would have been appalled to think I was suggesting he was discriminating against me.

But he was.

Everything the chief executive had been taught – from

the world he grew up in as a child to the images he now saw daily on TV, in advertising and even on the walls of his own office – had led him to identify the man in the good suit, with the good watch, as the person he felt more comfortable negotiating with.

Not the redheaded woman in a leather jacket and necklace so statement it could have decapitated a small child.

This drip, drip, drip of unconscious gender bias is around us all the time.

When two professors at Columbia Business School and New York University gave their students the same case study about a venture capitalist to read, there was one vital difference: gender. Half the students were told the venture capitalist was called Howard and half that she was called Heidi. Students rated both 'Howard' and 'Heidi' equally competent, but Howard was described as likeable while Heidi was seen as selfish and not 'the type of person you would want to hire or work for'.

So here we have some of the most educated students in the US assessing the same level of competence and achievement. And yet Howard is a good guy but you wouldn't want to give Heidi a job or have her as a boss.

Gender bias affects us in many ways. Sometimes we don't get the job, full stop – as with the orchestra. And at other times, even though we're doing a great job, we're not even considered to be competent at it.

The writer Catherine Nichols got so sick of being rejected by literary agents after sending out the first few pages of her novel with a covering letter, she decided to send it again – using a male name. And while her own name had netted her just two requests from fifty literary agents to see the full manuscript, seventeen wanted to see 'George's' work.

'He is eight and a half times better than me at writing the same book,' Catherine concluded.

I thought all that had stopped with George Eliot back in Victorian times.

Elsewhere, in the tech world, another study has found that computer code written by women is rated better than men's – but only if the people judging the work don't know it was written by a woman. If they do, they're less likely to approve it.

Even Google's algorithms don't think we're up to much. Have a go at typing 'CEO' into Google Images. I did and found four female faces in the first twenty pictures. One was Kylie Jenner's. Two others belonged to women patiently listening to a man talking in a meeting.

The search engine also displays six times fewer adverts for high-paying executive jobs if it thinks you're a woman.

All this hidden bias can come as a rude shock when young women enter the workplace. Of course they might have been aware of gender bias as a concept at school, but are often unencumbered by the reality of how it plays out at work. Then they get a job and discover that all is not quite what it seems.

Forget the good old days of overt sexism and discrimination. This is far subtler – because it's usually unconscious. We have to assume our dads, brothers, male friends and life partners don't want us to be disadvantaged at work. They want the best for us and to see us fulfil our potential and enjoy successful careers. So what's going on?

Researchers call it second-generation gender bias, a series of seemingly innocent actions that combine to reflect 'masculine values and the life situations of men who have dominated in the public domain of work'.

In other words, it's what men already 'know' about how the world of work operates because it's what they're implicitly taught from birth and what they then see playing out around them.

So, if corporate networking goes on in the pub after work and you're a mother who needs to get home for childcare, or all the supervisors at the factory where you work are men who play in the same football team, you're staring at second-generation gender bias.

It's about what's perceived as the norm – and subtly excludes all those who don't fit into it. No one's being outright rude, no one's telling you that your face doesn't fit. But it's in the ether around you.

Let's rewind to the beginning of my career when I started doing freelance display for a range of fashion shops after leaving Harrods. With no boss, I negotiated my own pay and managed my time. Busy driving around London in a yellow Spitfire and falling in love with my future husband, Graham, I didn't take much notice of how the world of work operated. I was doing well, I thought.

I was also enjoying myself after a tough few years following my mother's sudden death from meningitis soon after I turned seventeen. My father died three years later, and their loss had cut adrift my brothers, sister and me. Work, as well as my relationship with Graham, gave me the structure and safety I craved . . .

But after eighteen months of freelancing, I apply for a job as display manager at Topshop's flagship Oxford Circus store. Graham, who works in the corporate world, thinks working for a big retail brand will teach me a lot, and I agree. I go for the job and get it.

It's the mid-1980s, the era of Thatcher, a booming economy and yuppies. Sales, margins and systems are driving Topshop but, luckily for me, the chairman of the Burton retail group that owns the store is a man called Sir Ralph Halpern, who keeps a close eye on the US.

Over there, money is being splashed on designer labels like Calvin Klein and Ralph Lauren. Meanwhile, younger brands are creating fun, experiential retail, and display is being combined with sound, smell, layout and lighting to create a brand experience. Stores like Limited, Express, Guess and J.Crew are innovating all the time.

Sir Ralph knows what creativity can bring to a business and pays close attention to what I am doing to fill some of the biggest windows on one of London's busiest shopping streets. I have the money and staff to do it – plus a love of theatre that makes these windows my stage.

I want to stop people in their tracks as they walk down grey Oxford Street. Wake them up as they pass by our windows.

Flamboyant pop star Marilyn is put on a glittery throne in a sea of pink netting with a live band playing behind him. Hot-air balloons made of pastel silk float through the windows with scarves, jewels and handbags cascading down from them. At Christmas, the windows are filled with 500 penguins on icebergs for a monochrome theme.

Sir Ralph's attention is caught and, as a maverick at the top of the pile, he can work in exactly the way he wants. Instead of honouring the hierarchy's long chain of communication that stretches upwards through all the managers above me, the chairman circumnavigates it.

Working in my small dark studio in the basement, I pick up the phone.

'This is the chairman's office. He would like to meet you outside the front windows to look at the new display.'

'When?'

'Now.'

I run up the stairs, race onto the shop floor and up the escalator with the music blaring and my heart racing. The chairman. The chairman? What does he want with me? I'm a junior manager. A no mark.

Racing out onto Oxford Street, I screech to a halt in my Westwood boots, bleached, backcombed hair waving in the wind, to find Sir Ralph standing in front of the windows in his Aquascutum coat with his entourage circling him.

'Yes, Sir Ralph,' one says.

'I agree, Sir Ralph,' another chips in.

'Absolutely, Sir Ralph,' a third interjects.

He turns to me. 'I like the way you've styled the window but I need to show more product. Add some mannequins.'

New mannequins will cost a lot. I have a budget. My window designs have been signed off by my manager, his manager and the one above him too. I can't just change the whole thing.

But Sir Ralph is the chairman. This is what he wants. And so I do it.

Soon Sir Ralph has started hauling me into director meetings to talk through my window designs, and I wonder what on earth I'm doing in that room. I don't understand 'business' or the language that is spoken there: profit forecasts, numbers, percentages, ROIs and margins.

Slowly, I learn it, and soon my ambition is sparked, even though I hadn't grown up dreaming of a 'career'. That wasn't really a word where I came from. Until now, work for me has been a question of financial survival – with the unexpected fun of bringing ideas to life in windows.

But at Topshop I realize that my creative work is as vital to the bottom line as every other element of the business because I start to scrutinize the figures and see how they are affected by what my team and I do.

And the more I am called into the room where the managers meet and decisions are made, the more I know that I want to be able to make them too. And that the only way I will ever be able to do this is by moving up. Promotion doesn't happen laterally. I won't get my voice heard just because I'm good at my job. I must climb the ladder.

I work harder and harder, making the most of the faith that Sir Ralph shows in me. In today's world, he'd be called my sponsor. He could spot that I had a flair for my work and wanted to use it to improve his business . . .

I did well. By the age of twenty-six, I'd been promoted to senior management as head of display for all of Topshop's key UK stores. Eighteen months later, I became head of national display with a team of about forty staff. I was progressing rapidly.

But, as I was soon to find out, woe betide anyone who doesn't play the game according to alpha culture's rules.

Sir Ralph could buck the system because he was so senior but I couldn't. And it was then that I got my first taste of the kind of subtle gender bias that I experienced again, so many years later, when I went to see that CEO to sell him Kinky Knickers.

I want the ground to swallow me. I am sitting in a senior management meeting and the man chairing it is staring at me.

A minute ago, there was a break in the business we were discussing and everyone started to chat – myself included. But as the noise level in the room rose, the manager, who is very senior at Topshop, singled me out. The whole room fell silent as he stabbed his finger at me. 'You're really going to have to learn how to behave in management meetings, Mary,' he sneered. 'You're not in your display studio now. This is a boardroom.'

My cheeks flame red. New to the senior management team, I am now a regular fixture in these meetings instead of an occasional passer-by, courtesy of Sir Ralph.

And I know the manager is behaving like this because he never liked the fact that Sir Ralph went directly to me about things. In this man's eyes, I do not know my place so he's now very publicly reinstating the hierarchy that Sir Ralph inadvertently disrupted.

Today, to use the technical term, I'd call out his small-minded, belittling bullshit. But this was about thirty years ago, when office humiliation was as accepted as smoking a B&H on the top deck of the bus.

And this kind of power-play is often still at work today, fostered by our devotion to linear structures – a.k.a. the career ladder.

Power doesn't filter through many organizations according to who is good at what job and who is doing it. It is acquired rung by rung in a rigid management structure, concentrated in one pair of hands at each level until you get to the top.

But by giving leaders so much power, alpha culture allows them to create attitudes according to their rules rather than a common purpose. If they are honourable, responsible and inspiring, the culture they create will reflect this. If they are raging egomaniacs, it won't work out quite so well.

The Topshop boss fell into the latter camp because he didn't want me stealing his thunder with Sir Ralph, and communicated to everyone that his behaviour was acceptable by belittling me in public – and no one dared challenge him.

I didn't either. I'd seen how precarious your position on this power ladder could be.

When I first arrived at Topshop, the head of national display was a gentle and very talented man called Lennie. Focused on delivering the best work, he couldn't have been less interested in building a power base.

Lennie didn't have the loudest voice or push his own agenda; he wasn't interested in gaining power and prestige, just doing great work with the people he worked with. He was subtly sidelined while those around him worked to move upwards. Sales managers rode roughshod over Lennie's ideas and undermined him by giving his team direct instructions. They pushed harder and shouted louder in an effort to keep power in their hands and appear 'stronger'.

In the end, Lennie got lost in the process, leaving a couple of years after I arrived, and the business lost a key asset simply because this gentle soul couldn't and wouldn't play to the alpha type.

Seeing what had happened to Lennie, I stayed quiet when the manager called me out in the meeting. But I was determined to stand up for myself elsewhere after being promoted.

Having grown up with three brothers, I was used to fighting my corner. But I soon discovered that this was easier said than done: work was a very different environment from the one I'd known at home. I wasn't sure how to play the power game here.

My male colleagues talked football scores, had pints in

the pub and shared jokes with the other male department heads. As men, they shared a cultural currency, a common language that I would never speak – and were able to enter the club almost invisibly and be heard. Call it the old boys' network or straightforward networking, it enables those with power to pass it on to successors who share their values.

I experienced my fair share of it at Topshop where managers, mostly male, would invite colleagues, also mostly male, out to lunch and leave me sitting at my desk. They'd arrive back with some 'great ideas of what we can do' with my display strategy.

How I longed to come back from a working lunch with Mandy, Clare, Janet and Cat and announce to them that we'd sorted out a great new approach for meeting their sales targets. It wasn't going to happen.

Or they'd saunter over to let me know they'd decided to shift a certain product that wasn't working. 'Sale' stickers were going up all over my windows because it had been decided over lunch.

This behaviour not only excluded me from the decision-making process but also subtly reminded me I wasn't a true part of the alpha club.

Cronyism is still alive and kicking today. And it means that the qualities and values of one tribe are those by which everyone else is measured – and thereafter placed in certain boxes.

You know the kind of thing I mean. Women are 'good' at tackling the more sensitive meetings or clients. Women are 'great' at being team players, rather than leading from the front. Women are 'fantastic' at sharing achievements rather than claiming them for their own.

This is not overt discrimination. There are laws in place to tackle that. But gender bias influences not just the ways in which we behave, but which skills and abilities are more highly valued than others.

All of this flew straight over my head at Topshop. I was too focused on my work, too driven, too worried about whether peg legs or ra-ra skirts were in or out to spend too much time worrying about all the stuff I thought I could do nothing about. I loved my job, the team I managed, the ideas and challenges. It all seemed more important than what I dismissed back then as petty office politics.

So, instead of questioning what was happening, I took the codes of the alpha workplace and, without thinking too much about it, made them mine. If I couldn't go out to lunch or talk about sport, I would find another way to be seen as an equal player.

Slowly but surely, I learned how to play the political game well: currying favour at a senior level to get my ideas through; blinding my opponents with what they understood – numbers – to back up my creative strategy; drawing on the lessons I'd learned when I lost my parents at an early age and a granite core of survival instinct had been drilled into me.

I was going to join the game and win.

4

Do We Want to Be Leaders?

'The late Kenyan Nobel peace laureate Wangari Maathai put it simply and well when she said, the higher you go, the fewer women there are.'
Chimamanda Ngozi Adichie, We Should
All Be Feminists

I am standing in the corridors of power. Literally. I am in the House of Commons, the division bell has just rung and MPs now have eight minutes to reach the lobby to vote. I'm stranded at the top of a staircase as they rush to get there.

It's a dark winter's night in late 2016 and the writer Jeanette Winterson is with me. As well as being a novelist, she also owns a shop in Spitalfields and is concerned about the impact that ridiculous new business-rate rises will have on small retailers. We've just had a meeting with business secretary Greg Clark to talk about them.

Walking into the House of Commons reminded me of a childhood so Catholic my mother once genuflected by accident in the cinema: she went down on one knee, like Pavlov's dog, the moment she stepped on the aisle.

Parliament, just like a church, is about much more than bricks and mortar: it encapsulates centuries of history and tradition.

As we stand on the stairs, pinned in place, looking at the politicians rushing below us, I have an idea. 'Let's count how many women we can see,' I say to Jeanette.

Now, this is hardly a scientific experiment. Let's instead call it a snapshot of a moment in time. Over the next few minutes, Jeanette and I count about 150 male MPs running to the division lobby. I lost track of the exact number – there were so many of them. But I still remember exactly how many women we totted up: nineteen.

Given that we are at the heart of British democracy, I think it says something about how it works.

Once again, women are under-represented: a record 208 female MPs were elected in 2017 but it's still not even a third of the total 650. And that's before we start drilling down into what type of woman is represented here and how broadly they reflect the make-up of the British population. Just 4 per cent of all MPs are women of colour, for instance.

The problem goes even deeper, though, with far fewer women sitting on powerful select committees, and even the journalists reporting on politics being predominantly male. The management, communication and decision-making processes in politics are very definitely alpha.

Critics say the way Parliament works is a key reason why few women are attracted into it. The hours are long, unpredictable and hard to combine with family life, for instance. Some 45 per cent of female MPs are childless compared to 28 per cent of male.

But while these factors contribute, I think the lack of women in the world of politics is about more than long hours or childcare. It's about a culture that's so combative and riven with personal attacks that the BBC's political editor, Laura Kuenssberg, was widely reported to have had a bodyguard when she attended a Labour conference, to protect her from activists who were outraged by her supposed bias against leader Jeremy Corbyn.

You need an extremely tough skin to get involved in politics and compete. And, for me, this relates to the bigger issue of women and leadership, not merely the ability to step up (which we have in spades) but the desire to do so. It requires a belief that the work we do will be recognized, and the voice we bring to the table will be heard.

Progress is certainly being made. Thanks to things like government reviews and campaigning groups like the 30% Club, women's representation at board level is markedly improving. We now hold 29 per cent of positions on the boards of FTSE 100 companies – compared to just 12 per cent in 2011.

It's certainly good progress but there are still many companies without women at the top in significant numbers – and in 2016 women of colour held a paltry thirty-seven of a total 1050 directorships in FTSE 100 companies.

Just listen to some of the excuses CEOs gave to business minister Andrew Griffiths when he asked them why.

'There aren't that many women with the right credentials,' said one.

'Most women don't want the hassle,' said another.

Other corkers can be summed up as follows: 'We've already got one of those' and 'All the good ones have gone'.

Amanda Mackenzie, chief executive of Business in the Community, said it read like a script from a comedy parody. And she's right.

So, yes, things are improving – but there's still a lot of work to do.

It's obvious that some of us want to be leaders but don't get the chance because of outdated attitudes.

But I also believe many of us don't *want* to be leaders because of a working culture that is hostile to our presence, and requires us to suppress who we really are and behave in ways that often don't feel comfortable. So there may be some truth in women not wanting the hassle but there hasn't been enough thought put into why that is, and far from enough work to change it.

That's why Jeanette and I counted so few women running along that lobby in the House of Commons. The world of politics is a particularly male environment prone to hard-nosed competition and aggression that women must engage in to have a voice. Many are put off – or not accepted.

Bending into the shape required to be a leader in alpha culture wastes a lot of energy. And if all those men rising to the top had to do the same, I'm sure some would be put off climbing there too. Or wouldn't get there at all.

I am sitting in the Harvey Nichols boardroom. It's 1993 and I left Topshop four years ago to become head of visual merchandising here – the only woman in the position at any of London's major department stores.

The boardroom is huge, dominated by a rectangular table surrounded by beige walls hung with equally beige art. I immediately forget what I've just looked at after I've glanced at it.

I have learned the rules of this room since I arrived here. Where you sit in relation to the CEO says everything about where you are on the ladder of power, for instance, and I've done well at moving up it.

Business mogul Sir Dickson Poon bought the store a

year after I arrived and appointed Joseph Wan to revitalize its fortunes. Soon I had taken over the marketing and PR departments in addition to visual merchandising, before being promoted to the board as overall creative director aged thirty-one.

It was a question of right time, right place. I had my fighting spirit and lots of ideas when Harvey Nichols needed new thinking. Then I used every trick I'd been taught about alpha culture to carry on climbing upwards. So, I networked not just for the store's sake but also for my own reputation, made some tough decisions about bringing work in-house by severing ties with respected – but expensive – external consultants, and took on extra work to prove that I was ambitious.

Remember those men and their lunches at Topshop? Now I'm the one pulling senior colleagues aside after meetings to privately build support for decisions I want to get voted through at board level. If I don't manage that, I take creatively radical decisions and see them through before anyone notices what I'm up to. I take calculated risks because I believe in what I'm doing and that has served me well.

Today the topic under discussion is the sacking of a senior member of staff. They're talented but prioritize client loyalty over profit and this has got them into conflict. Our business is focused on the bottom line. Profit is the number-one priority.

My business brain agrees the sacking is the right decision. Every square foot counts. It's what I've learned throughout my career in retail. As tough as it is, surely this is what must be done.

But, deep down, something bothers me.

It's not that I believe people should be carried endlessly.

I'm certainly prepared to sack staff who aren't doing their jobs properly. (I still am today.) But this staff member has many years of valuable experience and is good at what they do. Surely there is a way to get them to focus more on the bottom line while still embracing their loyalty to their team.

I do not voice my doubts, though: fear is buried even deeper than uncertainty. For all that I can fight my own corner, strategize and survive in this highly competitive environment, I am also very aware of my place in it.

Just one board member is speaking up for the employee under threat: a man of about my age whose father is friends with the chairman. His voice is steady as he argues against the dismissal.

There are other men like him at this table but I am far more cautious. As a working-class woman, I have had to learn how to negotiate the codes in this room, how power is played and the external signals that I must give off simultaneously to respect the hierarchy and be tough enough to keep my position in it.

It's like a suit of armour I now wear: lunches at San Lorenzo, a designer wardrobe, and my previously bleached-blonde hair has been restyled into a classic copper layered bob. I also keep a pair of flat shoes in my desk to put on during meetings with particularly short male colleagues. (That is not a joke. I actually did.)

I have copied the identity of this place, made it mine, and the changes to my appearance have been mirrored inside me. I've always been tough but today I'm more driven and competitive than ever.

There is still the scrappy kid inside me, the one who was always getting into trouble and loved her family so much she was ashamed of her embarrassment about bringing her grammar-school friends – the ones with big houses and ponies – home for tea to her three-bed semi. But the acting ability I honed at school has served me well in this environment. Gender and class collide here and I have had to learn how to disguise both.

The men I work with went to the right schools. They have that innate air of confidence, born of an education that taught them they would be listened to and become leaders.

And they have also been bred to decipher all the tiny social cues: when to stand up as someone enters a room to show deference, or stay seated to signal they're equal. What watch to wear and which car to drive. What wine to order and whose son is on which cricket team with whom.

I have had to learn all this and more to maintain the illusion that I am one of them. I have to hide in plain sight.

So I do not speak of my misgivings about this sacking. In fact, I don't even allow them to become fully formed thoughts in my own head. Because at this stage of my career, I believe this is what I must do: show that I am tough and uncompromising; respect the hierarchy; demonstrate my complete loyalty – even to a decision that sits uneasily with me.

I should have spoken up, of course. Today I would. But back then I was unable to admit, even to myself, that I was afraid of opening up the debate. I was a fighter. I was brave. I didn't get scared. Did I?

In my experience, this is the multi-layered reality of being a woman at the top of business: containing many different selves, showing only one externally.

And this question of identity is, I believe, crucial to what slows women down on the way to the top. It's why, in so many cases, we aspire to leadership but don't actually *want* to become leaders because of who we have to become.

The question of identity is critical to women and leadership but it's the one we talk about least because it's so hard to define. Identity is personal. How can we measure the emotional twists and turns that those who don't fit into our dominant working culture must make? The permutations of gender, class, ethnicity, physical mobility, sexuality and personality are endless.

A white middle-class woman is one step removed from the alpha ideal of a white middle-class man so she's got to breach the distance of gender to fit in. A black middle-class woman is two steps removed as she's got ethnicity and gender to cover. An Asian working-class gay woman is really swimming against the tide.

'Making up' for all these differences from what's the accepted norm takes a lot of energy. We must be 'feminine' enough to be likeable – not too 'bossy' or threatening – at the same time as pumping up more 'masculine' emotions to be seen as competent leaders.

It's exhausting. I should know. I fell into the classic trap on this one at Harvey Nichols, where I drew far more on being competitive and tough than empathetic and collaborative.

The work culture we should be building is one that will allow us to be ourselves – not have to adhere to the expectations of another tribe to make real progress up the career ladder.

And yet in a survey of 2000 working women, three-quarters admitted changing how they looked or behaved to succeed. A quarter said they dressed in a masculine way, and half felt compelled to hide their true emotions. More than a third felt it was impossible to 'be nice' and reach the top, while a fifth felt that women had to act ruthlessly to be respected at work.

Stop for a minute and think about it. Who are the people you see most of the time being interviewed on the TV, in papers and on the radio? Who are the women in the public eye who really inspire you to think that you, too, can lead in an authentic way?

I bet that was a short brainstorm.

Of course, with fewer women leaders, pure numbers are working against us when it comes to being visible.

But, uncomfortable as it is to admit, unless you're glued to the broadsheet business pages, the women we do see or hear are often those who are attractive and young enough to make the pages of a magazine. Like it or not, if you're a woman in any area of the world of work – from a corporation to a cooking show – you are far more likely to be publicly profiled if you look good on a page or screen.

If you're in any doubt about that, just take a look at the journalists who get onto our screens: the women are all glamazons while many of the men aren't exactly lookers. Women's physical currency is still valuable in a way that men's is not.

If I could do anything to change young women's notion of leadership, I would ban those 'I-get-up-at-4.30-a.m.-do-aerial-yoga-before-working-on-my-peace-initiatives-feeding-my-five-children-and-perfecting-my-Mandarin-Chinese-in-the-car-on-the-way-to-a-7-a.m.-meeting-at-my-global-business' interviews that we so often see. Usually topped off with a photograph of a woman looking so perfect she'd probably crack if she got a spot of rain on her.

I think it's supposed to be inspiring but I just feel exhausted when I read about what they've done by 7 a.m. And I think the identities our women leaders sometimes adopt can alienate other women. One in four women says the senior women in her organization conform to a dominant and controlling 'alpha' type. So tightly controlled and 'professional', she can't relate to them.

Let's not knock the sisterhood, but I can kind of see their point. There *are* women who ape men's behaviour at work. There are also those who use their femininity like a stiletto knife wrapped in a Furby. If work is a battleground, then some women at the top are undercover agents using any disguise necessary to infiltrate the top ranks.

And all this leaves younger women in particular feeling confused. Who can they be and what identity can they aspire to if they don't relate to the most visible identities, if they can't be who they really are?

Role models are crucial to breaking this cycle. By informing, and indeed changing, our understanding of what it is to be a female leader, inspiring women at the top will help younger women believe they, too, can access the identity of leadership, and that identity doesn't take only one form.

We need to see more strong, vital, powerful and intelligent women.

Women like Cressida Dick, the straight-talking and cool-headed commissioner of the Metropolitan Police, who oozes no-nonsense wisdom whenever I hear her speak. Or Jayne-Anne Gadhia, chief executive of Virgin Money, who is not afraid to speak up on anything from her mental-health problems to the 'dinosaurs' she's encountered in business.

These are the women who should be on our TV screens and in the pages of newspapers and magazines. They should be heard on radio and be seen all over talk shows, wheeled out to turn on the Christmas lights – whatever it takes to make them, their humanity and wisdom more visible.

All the research papers and action plans in the world won't change women's access to leadership until we tackle the central question of identity: who we are, how we want to lead and what we aspire to.

And we're only going to do that when we stop acting like so many of the men around us and start being honest about who we really are.

5

Mind Over Matter

*'All human knowledge thus begins with intuitions,
proceeds thence to concepts, and ends with ideas.'*
Immanuel Kant

Picture the scene. I am standing in front of Harvey
Nichols's Christmas windows: metre upon metre of glass
frontage used to lure shoppers into the store. It is early
November and the windows have just been unveiled – the
most critical of the whole trading year. They are the jewel
in any department store's crown, the most intricate, colourful and expensive displays of the year.

Harrods, our closest competitor, is strung with so many
lights it looks like a space ship about to take off. Elsewhere,
I know without even seeing them that the windows of other
big stores will contain everything from a scene from *The
Nutcracker* to Santa's present-filled Arctic lodge.

It's the same thing year in, year out.

So what have I decided to do with the Harvey Nichols
windows this year?

Well, there are certainly no elves, fairies or Christmas
stockings. In fact, there's not really much of anything.

The only thing in our windows is a solitary light bulb

hanging in the centre, surrounded by a gaping black – and very empty – hole.

What I've done is radical. Some might even call it reckless. As vehicles for selling stuff, these windows are not exactly fit for purpose.

The only other prop in each one is a small sign telling shoppers what charitable cause the money that would have been spent on creating the Christmas displays has gone to support: someone sleeping rough or a child in need, for instance.

Harvey Nichols shoppers won't get expensive fantastical snapshots of Christmas. Instead, they'll know we're supporting those who can't afford to celebrate in the way our customers can.

So how did the idea go down with my colleagues when I first came up with it?

I'd say it was a dead heat between a cup of cold sick and a lead balloon.

'We can't do that!' they cried. 'We're a luxury business! Those windows will make our customers feel guilty!'

But I was nothing if not determined. And maybe a touch headstrong.

'We need to make Harvey Nichols unique, a destination,' I replied. 'We need to be innovating and doing things first. Imagine what people will say. We help charity and also get people talking.'

By garnering support person by person, I got the decision voted through at board level, and the empty Christmas windows were installed.

But although it was risky, I somehow felt sure it would work. Call it gut feeling or instinct, but my job was about influencing behaviours and getting people into the store through display, marketing and publicity. And if Christmas was the busiest, glitziest time of year then surely the most effective way of getting noticed was not to mimic what others were doing but to create something completely new. A talking point.

I was right. By Christmas Eve I could breathe a sigh of relief: the windows had got us noticed, we'd done good business and people very much in need were supported by the money we donated.

But what I realize now was that what made me so successful at Harvey Nichols – my intuition – flew in the face of alpha culture's devotion to logic. Because however fully paid up I was as a member of the alpha tribe, there were certain parts of me that couldn't be filtered out. And I drew on my intuition again and again to create windows that pushed the boundaries and helped revitalize the store's reputation.

I'd always been interested in art and culture but now melded it with shop display to create something new. To showcase the 'new neutral' grey and cream collections, I re-created 'Carhenge' – an installation of old cars spray-painted grey and stacked to look like Stonehenge in Nebraska – as a backdrop to the new season's fashions.

How I smiled as Pete the scrap-metal man and his crew wheeled beaten-up old bangers on pallets across the luxury floors of Harvey Nichols to install them.

'All right, ducks?' Pete said, to some old duchess who was buying a Fendi scarf.

When the now famous designer Thomas Heatherwick was just out of college, I commissioned him to create a wooden seascape installation that was laid over the windows – externally as well as inside. Admittedly, it somewhat flew in the face of the rule that all the action takes place behind the glass, and the pen-pushers at Westminster Council almost blew a gasket. They even threatened to close us down as they worried about the health-and-safety risk. What if a piece of the installation tripped up a Knightsbridge gent? It didn't.

Those windows were nothing to do with fashion. They were almost anarchic. But they got us noticed.

Renowned critic Brian Sewell wrote that the best installation art was to be found in the windows of Harvey Nichols. And shoppers, who back then had largely forgotten department stores in favour of the big bling designer shops on Bond Street, started to talk about Harvey Nichols again.

The early 1990s was also an era defined by money and ostentatious display, and I instinctively felt people would respond to something that played with this. Taking culture out of galleries and putting it into shop windows was one way to do it, poking fun at consumerism another. That was why I decided to position Harvey Nichols – best known as a luxury designer fashion store – in a TV programme that ruthlessly satirized luxury designer fashion.

When the designer Betty Jackson told me about a friend who had just written a new TV comedy that was going to be a send-up of the fashion industry, I knew it was an opportunity not to be missed. 'Will you introduce me to her?' I asked.

It felt like the right moment. As much as I loved – and still love – fashion, I'd also learned by this stage of my career just how deathly seriously some in the industry take themselves. And if the endless obsessing about fashion perplexed me – and I worked in it – then it would surely perplex others.

I decided to do what I'd done with the windows: play against type, make a counterintuitive move. I was intrigued by the show and arranged to meet the writer and make her an offer. I'd give her whatever she needed, from using the store for filming to having clothes on loan for costumes.

The woman was Jennifer Saunders. The series was *Absolutely Fabulous*.

Of course I had no idea what *Ab Fab* would come to mean, how it would capture the zeitgeist. But what I did know was that getting involved seemed like a way to have some fun, play with received attitudes to fashion and position Harvey Nichols in a different way.

Absolutely Fabulous was not just a hit but a phenomenon. It captured a moment of excess – and a fair whack of pretension – and made 'Harvey Nicks' as famous as 'Bolly'. Patsy and Eddie shopped with us, got clamped outside our doors, appeared in a fashion show in store and created a match made in Heaven between us and them.

And the decision to be part of a show that made a joke of fashion ironically turned us into a global destination.

But it was then that the clash between my instinct and alpha culture's logic started to make itself felt.

My strategies, along with the work others were doing in buying and sales, had raised Harvey Nichols's profile and revenues. And the moment that happened, the financial people were trying to pin down in numbers what was making us successful.

Financial acumen, as we all know, is certainly crucial to any business. There is no business without it. But although it's critical, it's just one part of a whole and, in my opinion, the people responsible for numbers often wield too much power – particularly when they not only want to understand what is happening by using numbers but, even more crucially, base most business decisions on them.

Again and again since then, I've seen the same thing: businesses run by such a ruthless commitment to the figures – with decisions based solely on statistics. In too many instances, it is fearful financial guardianship that has killed the soul and uniqueness of so many businesses.

But whether you're running a corner shop or a global enterprise, you can plan a huge amount based on what you know as fact: your market, profit margins, staffing costs and all the rest. After that comes intuition. Or instinct. Or whatever you want to call it. Sometimes you just know a decision is right even if you can't prove it – and the skill of trusting your instinct is often highly underrated in business.

Far greater minds than mine have talked about intuition's power in many areas of work. When a former head of GCHQ was interviewed about putting more women at the top of the intelligence services, he commented on the effect they have: 'it's radically different with two women on the Board rather than one,' he said. '[. . .] I find that the Board operates in a different way and I find that the discussions are deeper, I think they are more emotionally intelligent, and, if you like, I think there is more intuition in the room.'

Li Edelkoort, arguably the world's most influential trend forecaster, upon whose every word cosmetic, fashion and design companies across the globe hang, also says it's key to what she does: 'I listen like a slave to intuition,' Edelkoort says. 'I train it like an athlete, thank it like an individual, and now I've come to believe that it's not even my intuition – it's the way the human body is linked to a bigger experience and context.'

Oh, Li. Why aren't there more like you running businesses? People who see that tapping into something bigger than you, me or the calculator is crucial to success.

Intuition is not a female thing: it's a human thing. And it has served some of our most iconic male leaders well. Steve Jobs said that 'everything else is secondary' and Bill Gates also attests to its power.

In my small way, I also know that I have made my biggest mistakes when I have not listened to my intuition. It isn't quantifiable. You can't pin it down in figures or strategize it. It just is.

And that clash between intuition and logic would become a key reason why I started to fall out of love with alpha culture.

The other was ambition.

Let's start with debunking one important ambition myth. Women, we're often told, aren't as ambitious as men.

What a load of cobblers.

Women are ambitious. Incredibly so. I can even prove it using the kind of data that those financial friends of mine love.

Project 28-40, the UK's largest ever survey of women in work, found that 70 per cent have the desire to lead. Another massive piece of research by global professional services giant KPMG found that we also share the same ambitions as men in many key areas.

Achieving organizational prestige? Tick. Being well rewarded financially? Tick. Doing something that is intrinsically interesting? Tick. Add in contributing to something that matters and working on something innovative.

Using data collected from FTSE companies that together employed more than 680,000 people, KPMG discovered that men and women share all these key professional ambitions.

That's a lot of data.

But however much we have in common, there are also often differences in what men and women want from work. Women, for instance, value personal growth, positive relationships and good life balance. We want to be successful in a way that's about more than money and status.

KPMG didn't seem to see this as a problem: 'Women are more demanding and wide-ranging in their definition of success than men,' said their 2014 report, produced with global business psychologist firm YSC and the campaigning group 30% Club.

The desire to integrate professional and personal growth has been called circular ambition, as opposed to the vertical ambition typical of the male career trajectory. And it's an incendiary topic. Just ask Kevin Roberts, former chairman of advertising agency Saatchi & Saatchi and head coach at its parent company, Publicis Groupe.

Sitting down for an interview with Business Insider UK in the summer of 2016, Roberts said he didn't spend 'any time' on gender issues in his agencies. He also dismissed sexual discrimination in the advertising industry as a non-problem – and the lack of women in leadership roles. Which is something he should tell all the women aspiring to be creative directors in ad land. They hold just 12 per cent of these roles in the UK and 29 per cent in the US.

But he also made, inadvertently, I think, some very key statements about alpha culture – and why it must change. I want to look really carefully at what he said because it made headlines and Roberts resigned. (He's now the chairman of Beattie Communications.)

'We have a bunch of talented, creative females,' he said. 'But they reach a certain point in their careers . . . ten years of experience, when we are ready to make them a creative director of a big piece of business, and I think we failed in two out of three of those choices because the executive involved said: "I don't want to manage a piece of business and people, I want to keep doing the work."'

So, clearly, the linear ladder of power isn't working for them.

But surely if that's the case, and Roberts and his peers really want to harness all this talent, they'd listen to what their women executives are saying and find a way to work that allows them to lead in the way they want to.

Instead, they seem to be hearing what the women say and ignoring it because it doesn't fit with their perception of what leadership is. For them, it means desk time, managing intricate power relationships and often lonely autonomy.

Radical thought, but is there a different way to do it?

Roberts also talked about Millennials – both male and female: 'If you think about those Darwinian urges of wealth, power and fame, they are not terribly effective in today's world for a Millennial because they want connectivity and collaboration. They feel like they can get that without managing and leading, so maybe we have got the definition wrong.'

He went on: 'So we are trying to impose our antiquated shit on them, and they are going: "Actually, guys, you're missing the point, you don't understand: I'm way happier than you."

'Their ambition is not a vertical ambition, it's this intrinsic circular ambition to be happy. So they say: "We are not judging ourselves by those standards that you idiotic dinosaur-like men judge yourself by."'

Bingo, Mr Roberts. You came at it from the wrong angle and dismissed very real issues of discrimination and women's desire to lead. But you also – again inadvertently, it seems – hit the nail on the head when you talked about the anachronism of today's working culture and the way it views ambition and leadership.

Women – and many men – *are* circularly ambitious. But it's not a deficit of ambition. It's an excess. It's an ambition for a fulfilled life – both inside and outside work.

We aspire to leadership and professional excellence on our own terms. We want to collaborate and lead by doing great work with our team instead of slowly being distanced from our core skills and the people we work with as we push the lonely path up the linear power ladder.

We also want to be happy in terms of connecting with the world at large, family, friends and interests. I'd say this would probably make us better at our jobs and more productive too.

Who wants their account to be worked on by a knackered copywriter with no notion of life outside the job? Wouldn't you prefer an engaged, creative copywriter, who is contented in all areas of their life – including work?

Roberts's comments caused a furore but something was lost amid the backlash: the interview revealed the struggle many of those at the top face to adapt themselves to the realities of today's working world.

Half of the employees at Publicis, Roberts's former company, were women, yet he admitted that the issue of circular ambition was something the organization couldn't 'figure out'.

So, while I do not agree with his dismissal of very relevant gender issues in the advertising industry, at least Roberts acknowledged an important one: circular ambition. Many will rail against the idea that women might want different things from men but the truth is that we often do.

It's time we were honest about it.

'Circular ambition' is not a dirty phrase. It's a highly desirable reality. It means we're people, in the fullest sense of the word, who bring all that passion and knowledge to the workplace.

And here is the reality: women and Millennials (two pretty significant groups) are saying, 'No,' to our current ways of working.

So, I think it's time to rebrand the concept. Instead of calling it 'circular ambition', let's name this desire for personal and professional success 'life ambition'. In that way we might start to refine the current narrow definition of ambition.

All this was lost on me, though, during my first years at Harvey Nichols. (Bear with me here. At this point in my career, I was too elbow deep in the alpha mindset to think very deeply about all of this. And, culturally, at the time women generally were just trying to make their mark and pretty much had to do that in whatever way was possible: the male way.)

Driving forward, I did not even consider that I might want to devote myself to something other than work. I socialized with my husband, family and friends but that was it. I didn't have time for hobbies, interests or more downtime. And I thought that was just the way it had to be.

Until, that is, I hit the tipping point so many of us do, the non-negotiable that forces many of us to confront the limits of alpha culture.

I had a child.

6

The Elephant in the Room

'I've yet to be on a campus where most women weren't worrying about some aspect of combining marriage, children and a career. I've yet to find one where many men were worrying about the same thing.' Gloria Steinem, Outrageous Acts and Everyday Rebellions

Let's go back to the boardroom. Outside the boardroom, in fact, where I'm making a phone call.

'I'm running late,' I whisper. 'Can you give them a bath and I'll be home as soon as I can?'

The weekly board meeting starts each Tuesday at 3 p.m. and I always hope we'll finish by six. That's three whole hours. Enough time to cook a turkey the size of two newborns or have a heart bypass operation.

But, even with the combined brains and talent that is the Harvey Nichols boardroom, the meetings always run over.

I'm lucky that I don't *have* to leave. I have a nanny, as well as a husband, on his way back from work, who can look after Mylo, who's two, and one-year-old Verity.

But, even so, I'm looking at a ten-hour working day. Surely it's enough.

Seemingly not.

There is nothing else for it. I pretend I need to pee and nip out to make a call rather than admitting I must phone home. Any other day you might find me surreptitiously picking baby sick off my collar or forcing myself to smile after yet another broken night's sleep.

Once I even managed to stagger in on time after cutting my eye when I smacked into a lamppost. I didn't see it coming as I rushed to make a meeting and turned around to see Mylo peeping up as he stood in the window of our house.

All I will say is this: a lot of energy went into maintaining the illusion that my home life evaporated as soon as I stepped into the office. And while this was more than twenty years ago, I think many women today would say the same.

By the skin of my teeth, and a lot of hard work, I've managed to combine my career with being pretty involved in bringing up my children.

That's not to say it's been easy.

I have done more than my fair share of turning up late, not turning up at all and forgetting class trips, only to rush into a corner shop near school and wonder if a bin bag with two holes cut into the sides could double as a waterproof.

But it's impossible to cover every base when you combine a career with motherhood. Even if, like me, you think you have a foolproof plan to make sure it all goes smoothly. I'd waited until I could afford a nanny to cover my unpredictable, and sometimes long, hours. I'd also made sure I was indispensable at work so that I couldn't be replaced.

Then I had Mylo and Verity in quick succession – just twenty-two months apart – because I figured a one-off period of just-about-controlled chaos was better than returning to normal and plunging back into disarray three years later.

Unsurprisingly, though, my strategy came unstuck. Because the one thing I couldn't plan for was how much I would desperately love those two little people – or how much my priorities would change.

Graham and I were certainly lucky that we could afford to pay someone to help us. My sister, however, had to get on the bus with her son in his buggy on the days her husband was using the car, do a fifty-minute journey, then push the baby to his granny's for the day, before she even started 'work' as a nurse.

But while combining work with my life was certainly easier practically, money didn't solve every problem. Knowing that my children were looked after didn't lessen the intense pull of home, the splitting of myself into two people – mother and worker – or the fact that my kids wanted to spend time with their parents, not a nanny.

These two elements – the practical and emotional – are the reality of working women's lives. (Working fathers, too, to some degree, but it's still women who are most often the primary caregivers.) And while I was better off than many when it came to the first element, I still couldn't escape the second.

Because even though I had childcare, I was still largely in charge of the minutiae of my children's lives in a way that my husband was not. Just like most mothers are. And being the primary carer for a child takes up a whole heap of head-space and emotion that being a secondary carer doesn't.

In 2017, a cartoon by the French artist Emma called *You should have asked* tapped into this issue and went viral. In her clever and pithy drawings, Emma depicted how most women are carrying the mental load when it comes to our homes and children. Men help when they're asked but are not as plugged into it all.

If you're the manager of the home, Emma said in her cartoons, you're ultimately responsible for and therefore thinking about all aspects of the task.

We already know women do more physical work: in both the UK and the US, we spend double the amount of time on housework and childcare as men do. And even if you're the main earner, you're still 3.5 times more likely to do all or most of the household work than male breadwinners. In fact, the unpaid work we do in the home is valued at around £77 billion a year.

But, as Emma highlighted, it's the thinking that really gets us, the mental energy required to plan and file away information on everything from vaccinations to food shopping and produce it at a moment's notice. My name was even at the top of the ruddy vet's contact list if the cat ever needed picking up.

Men certainly pitch in but they aren't usually doing all this thinking about the thousands of details that make up running everyone's life. A friend of mine recently left her husband in charge of their seven- and ten-year-olds when she went away. She also tacked up a schedule on the wall of where everyone needed to be, when, with what food and clothing on, so that just about every waking minute was accounted for.

'Looking after kids isn't that bad, is it?' her husband said, when she got home. 'It's quite easy, really.'

Well, it is when everything apart from going to the lav is written down for you.

And, in my experience, physical care eases as children get

older but the mental load increases as the questions and emotions get more complex.

Men today are, of course, far more involved in their children's lives than a generation ago. Both American and British fathers have at least tripled the time they spend with their kids over the past fifty years. But they're also paying a price for how we divide up paid and unpaid labour.

One really interesting piece of research from the US found that men's psychological well-being and health gets worse the more financial responsibility they take on – while women's improves. Apparently it's because men are expected to do that stuff and feel the pressure to perform, while women are going against the grain by being a family's main earner and are admired for doing it.

'The psychological experience of being a breadwinner for men and women is really different,' said sociologist Christin Munsch. 'Men don't get any Brownie points for being a breadwinner, it's just the status quo. If they lose that, it's seen as an emasculating, bad thing – you're more likely to get teased by your peers saying your wife wears the pants in the family, that sort of thing.

'For women, being a breadwinner is not the expectation, so when you are a breadwinner, people look up to that. And if you lose that, you don't become a loser, it's just the status quo.'

It's clear that men face their own challenges. But what Emma was saying, and I certainly agree with it, is that women usually carry the mental load when it comes to our families.

And it's not just mothers. It's all women, whether they have children or not, because we're usually the carers. When elderly parents are sick or a friend is diagnosed with an illness, we are the ones who turn up, tune in and get stuff done. Children or not.

This is the mental load. And – single dads aside who are doing all this too – women usually carry more of it. Fact.

This is what I call the elephant in the room: it's taking up a lot of space even as we're mostly pretending it isn't there. Because while there's been revolution in terms of women's participation in paid work, there hasn't been one in the unpaid work we do at home after we have children. We are effectively now doing two jobs: one at home and one in the workplace.

Before children, we live pretty equal lives to men. Then we give birth and often wake up in the 1950s. Whether we're working or not, we're still mostly in charge of the home, kids and, increasingly, elderly parents.

Research suggests, though, that gay couples share both domestic work and childcare more equally. One study from the US found that 74 per cent of same-sex couples shared the responsibility compared to just 38 per cent of hetero-sexual couples.

The reason is that same-sex couples seem less hemmed in by what they 'should' be doing because of their gender. Heterosexual couples will often assume the roles they've seen their father and mother play during their childhood, almost by default, conditioned to see putting on the washing-machine as female labour while doing the DIY is male, for instance. Gay couples do not replicate that model in the same way. When it comes to housework, say, there's less 'You mow the lawn while I do the dishes' and more a div-ision of tasks according to who wants to do what.

What I'd like to see, of course, is a world in which the unpaid job of caring and the consequent mental load are equally shouldered. But we're far from there right now and, despite a lot of chat back and forth about this issue, it feels like much of it is nothing more than lip service.

Some businesses are doing great work to try to make caring for our families a more shared load but, once again, it comes down to the culture we're working in. We're still far away from living and working in a way that does not just accept but truly accommodates employees' role as carers and, because women are doing more of this, it disproportionately affects us.

Alpha culture still seems to view having children as a career obstacle – rather than the vital job it is – and puts taking time off to do it in the same bracket as a week in Spain. Until it adapts, I doubt many men will take over the job – or even share it equally with women – even if they want to. Far too often, it's still considered career suicide for a man to work flexibly or take more than the standard paternity leave. The way we work ultimately forces one person to be the primary carer – and it's more often than not a woman who pays a price in terms of earnings and promotion.

When it comes to caring, alpha culture is working against us all.

I'm pretty sure all of these issues would have been ironed out long ago if men were the ones caring primarily for children. How is it we have a tax system that allows businesses to write off first-class flights for their executives but doesn't allow someone who is self-employed to claim a penny for childcare? Ask a single mother if turning left on a plane or having her child looked after while she works is a more crucial business expense and I think we all know what the answer would be.

Or talk to the female commuter who works part-time and can't get a part-time season ticket on the train so ends up forking out more money proportionately on travel.

The irony, though, is that working mothers should be a force to be reckoned with. And businesses that aren't understanding this – and acting on it – are missing a trick. After all, English mothers with kids at home have seen the largest increase in employment rates over the past twenty years. Nearly three-quarters of mothers now work and there are fewer and fewer stay-at-home mums – both because women want to work but also because the cost of living has increased to the point where, for many couples, it's no longer an option to survive on one salary.

But here's the rub: until our children are eleven or older, we're more likely to work part-time than full-time, and the hourly rate for part-time work tends to be lower than that for full-time. Part-timers don't see the same kind of year-on-year salary increases that full-timers do either.

This – plus the career breaks we take to care for kids (and, of course, the mental load we carry for our families) – means we're often stuffed when it comes to earnings and promotion, and therefore pensions too. Yet we put up with it almost uncomplainingly because it's 'normal'. You make a choice to work or not to work, it's argued, with little regard for how the system penalizes women who do.

Lower pay and career breaks are key drivers of the topic that was on everyone's lips as I wrote this book: the gender pay gap.

Let's start by making it clear that this is a separate issue to equal pay. It's technically illegal to pay women less for doing the same job as a man. But it's also a grey area. Everyone, from female care workers to TV presenters, has argued that they are getting paid less for doing the same job as male colleagues.

Meanwhile, the gender pay gap is about the difference in median pay – the mid-point between the highest and lowest – of men and women in an organization. This means it gives a pretty good snapshot of the dynamics of the workplace: the bigger the gap, the more one earns compared to the other on average – which usually means more men are at the top earning bigger salaries and more women are at the bottom earning smaller ones.

Remember what I said about power, where it lies and how it affects our lives?

The UK's average gender pay gap for full- and part-time workers is 18 per cent. But when the government forced companies with 250 employees or more to release data on their gender pay gap in 2018, we discovered that there are also huge variations within this figure. Bonuses for female investment bankers at Barclays were 78 per cent less on average than those of their male colleagues. Across the bank's international division as a whole, women were earning on average about half what men earned.

EasyJet's gender pay gap? 52 per cent. Why? Because most pilots are men and they earn the biggest salaries. Phase Eight fashion retailer? A whopping 65 per cent. Low-paid shop workers are mostly women, while men do more of the more lucrative head-office jobs.

My heart dropped when I read those results. It's just unbelievable. And then I read that the World Economic Forum predicts the economic gap between men and women won't close in Western Europe until 2078. And my heart dropped a little more. That's about the time my daughter Verity will retire. I've told her often that she can be and do anything she wants but she will never see economic parity in her working lifetime.

So just to recap: over the past fifty years, we've managed to fight several wars, map the human genome and use the internet to revolutionize everything from how we fall in love to telling us when the milk's about to go off in the fridge.

Yet we haven't sorted out women's pay?

To say it's complex is an understatement. But, in a nutshell, lots of long and complicated defences are given for the gender pay gap: men do more overtime and qualify for more bonuses, for instance (which begs the question: why are they able to do those extra hours?); it's a meaningless statistic based on bad data.

But given that girls are now outperforming boys in education, surely something is going seriously wrong if they end up so consistently worse off in the workplace. Men who are less qualified are quite simply moving higher up the ladder and earning more. Women are disadvantaged whichever way you slice and dice the data.

And I'm off for a lie-down before I explode.

7

The Rock?
Or the Hard Place?

*'Women with their caring and sharing will be
the teachers of how to be human in the future.'
Vandana Shiva, scholar, author and activist*

It's not physically having children that affects women's careers. It's being the main carers for them that, in many cases, stuffs our chances of progression and earning.

I'll jog right past the fact that as many as 54,000 pregnant women lose their jobs each year because of unfair and unlawful treatment. I'll also swerve criticisms of our statutory maternity pay as among the lowest in Europe. Instead, I'll fast-forward to the part where we've given birth, taken time off and want to get back to work. The longer we're off, the harder that's going to be because, in the fast-paced world of alpha culture, we're often seen as irrelevant when we've had time out – despite the skills we've acquired along the way: multi-tasking, an ability to look at the bigger picture and keeping a cool head under intense pressure.

If that CV gap is a barrier we can overcome and we return to work, it's likely to be in a less skilled and lower-paid post than we held before we had children: three in five mothers are at risk of this – and will earn up to a third less. As we know, we're also more likely to work part-time.

The effect all this has on women's earnings is there in black and white. Younger women now out-earn younger men but the gender pay gap starts to open after we hit forty, when many of us have dependent children. It's widest by the time we're in our fifties, and the average woman will be earning almost a third less than the average man twenty years after having her first child.

But wait for this.

The real kicker is that many men's wages rise when they become fathers. Apparently it's because they often put in increased hours and effort, particularly when their female partner reduces her hours, but also might be because they're seen as more committed and responsible.

So there we are: dropping our hours to care for kids, grappling with everything from sleep deprivation to loneliness, impacting our future earning potential, and our male partners are getting pay rises.

The depressing moral of the story is this: if you're a woman who wants to keep up with men's earnings, don't get married or have kids. That is the painful truth.

So how do we solve all this?

Well, there's no getting around the fact that women give birth to children and, aside from the superwomen who are speed-dialling the office even as the gas and air is wearing off, most of us want time at home to recover physically, get into a routine and bond with our baby. Breastfeeding is also a physical tie.

But once that's done, we need to help women get back to work more quickly – and good-quality affordable childcare is key to doing this.

Sounds easy, doesn't it? It's not.

Childcare in the UK is among the most expensive in the

world. For instance, British parents spend a mind-boggling eight times more of their income on childcare than Swedish parents. Childcare costs have risen four times faster than average pay since 2008. And there aren't enough nursery places so thousands of grandparents – particularly grandmothers – are filling in the gaps.

Those working outside a normal nine-to-five pattern, like nurses or shop workers, face even bigger problems finding a place because most nurseries work Monday to Friday and close at 6 p.m., and less than a fifth of areas have sufficient spaces for disabled children.

In 2017, the UK government put a record £6 billion into childcare funding and introduced new policies, including thirty hours of free childcare per week for working parents, who earn less than £100,000 per year, of three- to four-year-olds.

But, despite the record investment, the UK's problems are far from being solved. Low-income parents are still struggling to pay – even with the free care they get. And providers are closing because the money the government pays them for the 'free' care doesn't cover what it costs to provide.

Meanwhile, the argument for improving childcare couldn't be clearer. If just 10 per cent more mothers worked, they could generate an estimated additional £1.5 billion for the UK economy. Universal free childcare could earn the nation up to £37 billion through higher tax revenues and lower benefit payments.

High-quality childcare also does children good. Those who have it in their early years do better emotionally, physically and economically – particularly if they're from disadvantaged backgrounds. That seems to me a good way to make society more equal.

But even though many of us are struggling with this situation every day – from finding a place to paying for it – we're not getting that angry about it. Instead, we're all beavering away uncomplainingly to pay childcare bills that parents in many other parts of the world don't have.

Fox-hunting got way more people frothing at the mouth than childcare provision ever has. And someone, some time, needs to explain this to me. Why haven't we been out on the streets marching in protest about it? Or, at the very least, demanded that our MPs take it a bit more seriously?

Everyone from France, Norway and Germany to Spain, Slovenia and Chile invests significantly more of their GDP in childcare than we do. They've been doing it for years because they believe it's money well spent.

The ultimate irony of our eye-watering childcare costs is also that it's mostly women on low pay who are providing it. Nursery workers must be qualified but may also be required to have anything from first-aid skills to knowledge of the kinds of nature activities that children do at a forest school. And what would they get paid for all this? £8 an hour?

A McDonald's 'crew member' aged twenty-five or over gets that to flip burgers.

Unpalatable as it may be, better-paid parents of both sexes are relying on poorly paid women to look after the home front. Collectively, we need to work out a way not only to put more money into caring for our children but also to pay properly the women who are doing the job because it's scandalously undervalued.

But, for now, one thing is pretty clear: women face huge employment barriers simply because they care for children.

To those who still try to peddle the old 'women-aren't-ambitious-after-kids' line, I say this: there will certainly be some women who self-limit, but I'm pretty sure they often do it because of the lack of affordable childcare – not because they suddenly want to get home early every day for a Monkey Music class.

Going up the ladder also usually requires more hours, mental commitment and stress. And I think we've got quite enough on our plates juggling all this, thanks very much.

Some women make it work. Of course they do. I am one of them. I didn't have any parents to help out or understanding bosses, but I was lucky to be successful early in my career and paid enough to afford at-home childcare throughout my children's lives.

But for many women it's often down to a large salary, or two good salaries, a lot of hard work, some good luck, an empathetic boss, a husband who's willing to pull his weight at home, and someone like a very involved grandparent who gives free care, or any combination of the above.

It means that our career outcomes are often based on chance because the structure that should be in place – from affordable childcare and more flexible working opportunities to a more positive culture around sharing care for children – isn't there most of the time.

And here's my thought: should our success as working mothers really be down to this kind of lottery? Some of us get a winning ticket thanks to all of the factors I've mentioned, but those who don't are held back.

Some will insist that after decades in the workforce we are now competing on equal terms and things would surely have changed if we really wanted them to. That women are somehow complicit in the status quo.

But it's hardly a level playing field, is it? We're playing with one foot tied to the other, as far as I can see.

And there are people who know exactly how it is for working mothers and are happy to perpetuate the situation. I was once at a working dinner with a man who'd had various chief-executive jobs during his career. As we discussed recruiting the best talent, he leaned over the table towards me. 'I like employing mothers,' he said, whispering conspiratorially, as if he was giving me the numbers for a winning lottery ticket. 'You pay them for three days and they're so conscientious, so worried about being accused of slacking, that they do five days' work in that time.'

I just managed to stop myself hurling my coffee across the table at him.

8

Going It Alone

'I love to see a young girl go out and grab the world by the lapels. Life's a bitch. You've got to go out and kick ass.' Maya Angelou

I was never at the coalface of childcare in the way so many women are. But, nevertheless, I was still trying to parent in a working culture that is often resistant to caring.

At the top of a very male-dominated industry, I had to keep going as if nothing had happened. I didn't have a choice about that. I was like the band that kept playing as the *Titanic* went down – only my ship had ear infections, school projects and nits on board.

My first pregnancy was spent working long hours on one of the most ambitious projects I'd overseen at Harvey Nichols. In Harrods we had a rival – just down the road – with far larger budgets and a global reputation as the ultimate store for luxury. What designer wouldn't want to see their products being sold in their marble halls? Once you got your product into Harrods, you could get into any store worldwide.

But losing out to the buying power of Harrods was a problem because having the best selection of luxury designer labels was everything in the 1990s. This was the era of the first supermodels – but also the first super-brands. Kate Moss was making Calvin Klein's Obsession iconic. Elizabeth Hurley stood on the red carpet in a black dress held together by safety pins – and catapulted Versace into the popular imagination.

The internet was a mere blip on a few computer screens – people were still a long way from buying online. The physical shop was king. Having exclusivity with certain designers made you a destination, and when stores struck exclusive deals with labels, it got people through your doors in search of them.

And while I might have created windows that had got people talking about Harvey Nichols, I now had to find a way to capture interest for its fashion credentials.

I knew there was a market to tap.

If Harrods was the fabulous *grande dame* of style, Harvey Nichols could claim a place as a more modern, contemporary department store. London's giant stores were many things at that time but cutting edge they were not. I had an idea that I felt sure would change everything and took it to the best in the business: Wendy Dagworthy, head of fashion at the Royal College of Art, and Louise Wilson, head of fashion at Central Saint Martin's. As two of the most influential mentors to aspiring design students, Wendy and Louise were also the most qualified to spot upcoming talent.

Those two formidable women, Harvey Nichols's buying director, Amanda Verdan, and I hand-picked the designers we believed would be tomorrow's stars.

The project was called New Generation and it would see Harvey Nichols put on young designers' shows during

London Fashion Week to give them much-needed exposure. If I could get our best British talent to show exclusively at Harvey Nichols, it would communicate that we were the store of newness, modernity and innovation. British fashion has always been about breaking new ground, and I was sure that showcasing this would place us at the heart of the fashion zeitgeist and capture a lot of interest.

The first show was staged on the fifth floor where a new restaurant, bar and food hall had been opened. It was a dramatic space and, to make the most of it, the catwalk had been positioned high above the escalator so that people could sit in the café and watch the show.

I was heavily pregnant with Mylo as I lowered myself into a chair to watch the then relatively unknown milliner Philip Treacy do a final run-through of his show, which was being styled by his friend, the legendary Isabella Blow.

Philip's collection was extraordinary. Those weren't hats. They were works of art.

Trouble was, most of them were also about two foot tall.

Sitting in the audience, I watched them rise off the models' heads – and crash against the rigging that had been set up for the lights above the catwalk.

'This will never work!' Isabella screeched. 'We can't do the show.'

For one awful moment I thought the whole thing would have to be cancelled and almost gave birth on the spot. Then I did what I always do: glided like a swan, smiled, reassured everyone, and paddled furiously underneath the surface to sort out the problem.

My wonderful team of carpenters worked overnight to lower the catwalk by six inches, the show went ahead and was a huge success. All the fashion press came – as did buyers from famous stores like Barneys, Neiman Marcus and Bergdorf Goodman. That, for me, was the greatest proof that my instinct had been right: our competitors were coming to our store to get inspiration. Magazine editors, the fashion establishment and influential buyers loved New Gen. It was such a hit that it's still running today as a key part of London Fashion Week.

But more importantly for Harvey Nichols back then, it also attracted big designer labels to the store: they wanted to piggy-back on the cool of our future fashion stars.

I loved the project and returned to work quickly after having Mylo to put on a second successful show, and did the same brief maternity leave with Verity. But my heart broke a little each time I packed away my brief spells of full-time caring because the gravitational pull of my children took my breath away.

Giving up work wasn't an option, though: my family relied on my income and, in any case, I *wanted* to return. But when I got back to my desk, I realized things had changed. Or, rather, I had.

For a start, I discovered how much time I'd been wasting for years. Serious amounts of it. The energy that had gone into networking, cajoling and building alliances. Coffees here, lunches there.

All of a sudden, none of it mattered much. Now I simply let my work speak for itself and became efficient with my time. I wanted to spend my mornings and evenings with my family. So out went most of the breakfast meetings. So did most of the lunches. I was usually at my desk by 9.30 a.m. and heading home by 5.30 p.m.

I still had long days during intense work periods but I'd dare say there is no worker more efficient than a multi-tasking mother. I could either waste time or spend it with my children. There was no decision to make.

It was still a constant internal struggle, though.

Arriving in Milan on a business trip, I opened my suitcase to find Mylo's cuddly penguin inside. I'd raced all over the house looking for it before having to leave him sobbing. He must have put it in my suitcase as I packed and forgotten where he'd left it. Now there it was, staring up at me as I sat in an empty hotel room about to go out for dinner with all sorts of fabulous fashion types while my gut wrenched for home.

Despite all this, the balance between the well-being of my children and my working life made sense for me personally until things also started to change at work.

Up to this point, you might be forgiven for thinking I had single-handedly saved Harvey Nichols, like the Joan of Arc of luxury retail. But I didn't. It was very much a team effort because that's when the best work happens – collaboration being the key word for me: the alchemy between people creates a magic that is more than the sum of its parts.

All of us on the board had a part to play.

Joseph Wan, the CEO, had the courage to get rid of dead wood, invest in the remaining team and give us the freedom to do the work we believed in.

Sales director Patrick Hanley was my mentor: at the time it was very unusual for someone to cross over from high street to luxury retail, as I did. He taught me to make alpha culture work for me by packaging ideas correctly, holding back deals until just the right time for maximum effect, and achieving the right balance between products that had profit margins and those that created cool. A big, fabulous Irishman, there wasn't a trick in the book he didn't know about retail. He was probably the best sales director I ever worked with.

Critically for alpha culture, Patrick also taught me the importance of how to make my seniors look and feel good. I might like seeing Harvey Nichols mentioned on the fashion pages but the CEO was far more interested in the financial ones. Patrick transformed the street fighter who arrived from Topshop into a gentlewoman boxer.

Then there was Amanda Verdan, the buying director, whose brilliant eye was the keenest in the business. She was so tapped into designers that most of them had her on speed dial as their next of kin. Part-French and super-stylish, she taught me how to dress by investing in classic pieces. Out went high-street looks that changed every second week. In came a great white shirt, a slim-line black trouser and a tailored jacket. Topped off, of course, with a bit of statement jewellery.

Gill Toal, the HR director, was not only supremely efficient but believed in all of us and our vision. We wanted to be the best and Gill enabled us to have the staff and structure to achieve it.

And, last, Dominic Ford, who was in charge of the restaurant, bar and food hall, and understood the role that food and drink play in all our lives. It's more than just a plate on the table. It's about coming together, being social and connecting with each other. He never once saw Harvey Nichols as 'just' a department-store restaurant. He wanted to compete with the best restaurants and chefs in London. And he did.

It was a really powerful group of people, which in many ways reminded me of my family: I might be the loudest in the room but no one felt threatened by me. I had my place.

My colleagues not only let me be me, they made me a better me because I admired them and wanted them to respect me back.

There was no power-playing. We simply came together at a time when the only way was up for Harvey Nichols, and while it's challenging when a business is faltering, it also offers huge opportunities. We had to do something bold to turn the store around and we did. Harvey Nichols claimed its place as London's hottest store.

But then Amanda left, the dynamics changed and certain things happened that started to take the lustre off what had been a golden time professionally.

While I was on maternity leave to have Verity, for instance, my number two was also off having a baby so our number three, Krishna Montgomery, took over. She didn't just keep things ticking over. She was so conscientious that when documents had to be biked to my house by courier, I wouldn't have been surprised if Krishna had turned up riding the Kawasaki herself.

I wanted to give her a bonus when I got back to work – the kind of bonus that would really show her how much her work was appreciated. But I was voted down at board level because it wasn't the time of year that bonuses were awarded. The computer said no. The rules of alpha culture couldn't be adapted in a human way.

At the same time, the Harvey Nichols numbers were growing, and the more they did, the more time I had to spend analysing them and justifying what I wanted to do in financial terms. Being commercial and hitting targets was important. But if finances alone created successful businesses, the whole corporate world would be made up of accountancy firms. (Oh. Hang on a minute. A lot of it is.)

I knew how things worked. I was realistic. I accepted that the men were all in offices on the top floor of the building (Gill was admittedly stuck on the end), while I was one floor down with my team and the buyers. I also accepted that the men lunched and chatted together in a way that felt at times as excluding as it had done at Topshop.

But when I found out that someone relatively new to the senior finance team was paid more than me, I discovered that my role wasn't as valued as the traditionally male provinces of sales or finances. I was the 'creative' one: useful but not *that* useful. I earned good money. But not as much as the men. I was respected. But not as much as they were.

The decision-making – and wages – was all about testosterone. And if a fashion business can't value creativity, I'm not sure who can.

There was an unseen barrier I would never get past, and my role would never be considered as important as that of the moneymen.

It's still a fundamental problem in many industries today because creativity isn't limited to those working in fashion, design or the arts. Creative thinking is central to any kind of business. It's what kick-starts big ideas, challenges the norm and the way of doing stuff.

What numbers would all the financial guys be crunching if I, and people like me, hadn't made Harvey Nichols a destination? And for all that work and dedication, I was being paid less?

I was incensed.

So I didn't leave my job because the dual role of executive and mother was too much. I left because it wasn't enough. The only solution was to start my own business and be in control of my own destiny.

But who leaves a high-paying, high-status job for the uncertainties and insecurities of starting a business when they've also got two toddlers rampaging around fighting over the Playmobil? I had a large mortgage, too, and was the main earner for my family. It wasn't just my life I was responsible for.

Nevertheless, my intuition told me I should leave.

If I was going to keep getting metaphorically patted on the head, I would work with people who valued what I did and set up a business that was all about skills, talent and innovation. Clients would come to me and pay for my thinking. I knew I could take the risk because I was good at what I did.

And, with that, my life as an entrepreneur started.

I set up my own business because alpha culture wasn't working for me, and other women seem to be doing the same.

Self-employment has been increasing ever since the global financial crash of 2008, and women have accounted for much of the rise. More and more of us are going it alone to better suit our needs. It's estimated that two million of us will be self-employed by 2019.

In the US, black and ethnic-minority women have really set the pace. They are now at the helm of one in three female-owned businesses – compared to one in six twenty years ago. Given that alpha culture is particularly tough for women of colour, it surely can't be coincidence that they are opting out of the traditional system in such large numbers.

The Global Entrepreneurial Monitor is the largest ongoing study of the subject in the world and produces a report each year looking at entrepreneurial activity in seventy countries. The 2016 study reported that for almost all new women entrepreneurs a key reason for starting their business was 'to have considerable freedom to adapt my approach to work'. Interestingly, about 80 per cent of men said the same.

There are many reasons to start a business. But if so many self-employed women are saying they want to adapt the way they work, then surely they are finding traditional employment – linear power, long hours and inflexibility – too limiting.

Despite the rise in women's self-employment, though, our full potential remains untapped because women are still only about half as likely as men to be entrepreneurs.

And, once again, there are barriers for us to overcome: from access to finance, to the fact that we're more likely to start businesses in lower-earning sectors, or a lack of affordable childcare.

Fully tapping into women's entrepreneurial talent would give the UK economy a massive boost. One estimate put it at £150 billion. That's an awful lot of money we're not seeing because women's full potential isn't being realized.

But while work is certainly happening to break down the inequalities and encourage women to self-start in business – from Facebook's She Means Business campaign to the Women in Enterprise Taskforce created by the Federation of Small Businesses – there is still much to be done, not least an honest appraisal of how tough self-employment can be.

I don't want to burst the entrepreneurial bubble but a lot of self-employed women are struggling to get by on low pay as cleaners, carers and delivery drivers. Women who are self-employed earn £243 a week on average compared to £428 in full-time employment.

That's the bad news.

But I also know from experience that it's possible to build yourself a great working life by running your own business – and get well paid. Passion isn't enough. You need some realism, too, and knowledge of your market: your devotion to cold-pressed yak milk doesn't mean you'll make anything like a living wage from it.

If you have a good idea (that's the tricky bit), a sound financial plan (not just for your business but detailed numbers looking at how you're going to survive in what can often be a long period of low profit) and the capacity for hard work, don't be put off.

People who work for themselves are more likely to feel satisfied than those in other employment and, if you're ready for the challenges, it offers many opportunities – not least creating a working world tailored to your professional strengths and personal needs.

You can work like a woman, if you choose. And that is a truly liberating thing.

9

Breaking the Codes

'Only the truth of who you are, if realized, will set you free.' Eckhart Tolle, A New Earth

For the first year after starting my own business, I spent a lot of time peering into a tin shaped like a red telephone box that sat on my kitchen shelf. Inside it was the money – in cash – that the four of us had to get through the week.

You return directly to 'Go' when you start up your own business. I was no exception. Gone were the big salary and perks. So, too, were the designer discount cards, restaurant lunches, the structure, the status and the nice office.

Instead I sat at a desk, loaned to me by the media agency PHD in return for project advice, which was opposite the lift. Everyone who got out of it thought I was the receptionist.

Failure, as they say, was not an option. The whole Portas family would be living in a box if the agency didn't work, because Graham had left his teaching job to join me, looking after its finances and administration.

When I set up the business in 1997 my vision was to help other brands and retailers do what I'd done at Harvey Nichols: engage with consumers in many different ways. That could be done via anything from an advertising campaign to a product launch, a marketing strategy or brand creation.

I'd saved to fund us through the first year of business because I knew I wouldn't take a salary. I'd also negotiated a three-days-a-week consultancy for Harvey Nichols to give me a reduced but steady income and was lucky to sign my first client before I'd even left my job.

When the managing director of Clarks shoes heard I'd resigned, he sent his marketing director to see me at Harvey Nichols. They signed with my agency when it wasn't even up and running. I'll always be grateful for the faith Clarks showed in me then and for the next eighteen years as my client.

So I had money to live off in the bank – as long as I tightly controlled business and personal expenditure – and free office space. A creative business like mine doesn't need a lot of investment at the beginning, in terms of product or infrastructure, so those were costs I didn't have to cover initially. I quickly acquired more clients, thanks to a good reputation and word spreading that I was out on my own. Within six months, I'd taken on four staff.

Setting up a business with two young children is tough. Really tough. Not just in terms of the time it takes, but the mental and emotional energy you must pour into it. This took its toll on Graham and me. Five years after starting the agency, we couldn't make our marriage work and decided to divorce.

The separation of a family is never without a lot of pain and change. The thought of building a new life for yourself without your partner is pretty terrifying. But mostly you're worried about what it might do to your kids.

Graham and I knew that divorce could get incredibly messy. So, way before Gwyneth and Chris consciously uncoupled, we determined to keep things as amicable as possible to ease the path for Mylo and Verity. We couldn't get caught up in our own stuff in a way that would damage them.

Key to that was making them feel as if they didn't have to 'pick' a side and ensuring they saw a lot of us both. We split our time with them straight down the middle. Graham stayed in our family home, I took on another mortgage to buy a new place, and Mylo and Verity spent alternate nights at each house. We bought two of everything so they didn't have to drag bags between the houses, and they saw Graham or me every morning or evening depending on where they were that day.

We did this for two years and I'd work like mad when they were with Graham to free me up when they returned to me. When Mylo started secondary school, we moved into a more traditional pattern of one night a week and alternate weekends with Graham. But I think that initial period really helped root in them the idea that they weren't losing either of us.

I will always be proud that Graham and I divorced as amicably as we did and concentrated on our kids. We did okay, I think.

But the following year, someone came into my life who would reshape it for ever, a person who forced me to rethink almost everything I thought I knew: a woman named Melanie. I met her at a working dinner and fell in love with her almost instantly. It really was as simple as that. It wasn't something I had anticipated or looked for. I certainly hadn't spent my marriage secretly pining after the woman in the nail bar or wishing I could take Linda Evangelista for a cocktail. But I fell in love with a person who happened to be a woman, and meeting Melanie thrillingly derailed so much of the structure that I had set up in my life – and where I believed I was going.

You don't go from being married to a man to being in a relationship with a woman – with two children to consider – without quite a lot of sleepless nights. It was a huge adjustment not only to how I lived my life but the person I'd thought I was.

Graham was the only one I told at first: I quickly knew that Melanie and I had a future together so at some point Mylo and Verity would be aware of that – and part of it.

We decided not to spell it out to the kids for now. Melanie lived around the corner from me and at first we saw each other when the children were with Graham. Then, gradually, she started to visit when the children were with me and bit by bit came more often, until they started to ask where she was when she wasn't with us.

So far, so good, until the day Mylo, Verity, Melanie and my very Christian au pair were sitting at the kitchen table while I cooked.

'How do you spell lesbian?' Verity suddenly squeaked, as she sat writing a card to a friend.

The blood drained from my face. How did a seven-year-old even know that word? I certainly hadn't mentioned it. And what was the bloody au pair thinking?

Mylo, nine, looked up. 'Verity is a lesbian now,' he said, with a heavy sigh. 'And she's told Daddy.'

I set my face to neutral. Was I giving off lesbian pheromones? Graham was going to wonder what on earth Melanie and I had been up to.

For once in my life, I was lost for words.

While I spelled out the word (which felt like it took about thirty-seven minutes), the au pair sat looking confused and appalled in equal measure and I slammed plates of pasta on the table hoping to divert attention.

But after we'd eaten, I picked up the card, curious to see what on earth Verity was up to. 'Dear Leah,' she'd written. 'I will so miss you when I go to my new school. You are like a beautiful sunflower and you make me happy. I love you. Verity.'

Then she'd added something at the end.

'PS Lesbian.'

I started to cry. I didn't know where she'd heard the word but Verity thought lesbian meant loving a girl.

And in a way, of course, it did.

In that moment, I knew my relationship with Melanie was as simple as Verity had made it. Melanie made me happy. It was time to have my own 'PS lesbian' moment.

It was then that I started to become more open about the change in my personal life. It didn't happen overnight but gradually my family, friends and, over time, Mylo and Verity understood that Melanie was Mamma's girlfriend.

For what it's worth, no one really batted an eyelid. Particularly the kids. Melanie pretty much seamlessly became a part of our family because children are way less bothered about the boxes we put ourselves into than we adults are. She played with the kids, talked to them and was interested in them. That was all that mattered. They had Mamma, Daddy and now Melanie. Later, Elisabeth would also join our family when Graham remarried. One of my happiest memories is of turning up to Mylo's carol concert with him proudly flanked by his 'four parents'.

All I'd say is this: there were challenges, but falling in love with Melanie forced me to take a risk that changed me very fundamentally. I'd lived according to the rules and now I was beyond them. The codes I'd adhered to had been thrown up in the air.

I didn't know it right then but that change in my personal life would in time be the foundation of changing the way I worked too.

And that, for me, was perhaps an even greater risk because work was the one thing I'd always clung to for safety and security. But my relationship with Melanie proved to me that I could cope with huge change – and flourish – and it was a vital lesson for the future.

For now, though, all that was to come and the change in my personal life still had to be negotiated professionally. Mostly, my relationship with Melanie went without comment. But while fashion might be more liberal than other professions it's also a small world and I knew people were talking.

At one meeting, a chief executive I knew well gave me a wry smile and alluded to it lewdly.

Another low was sitting next to a well-known tycoon at a charity dinner. Just before I went on stage to give a speech, he turned to me and said, 'Tell me, Mary: how do two women ****?'

Classy.

Remember those layers of distance from alpha culture that I talked about earlier? My new relationship had added another and the power dynamic had shifted.

It was perhaps the first time I realized just how powerful straight male/female dynamics can be at work: the jokes, the subtle flirtations. Now that I was a gay woman, some of the most powerful men in my working world didn't seem to know what to do with me. And the only thing some could come up with was really offensive jokes.

(PS You don't need to fall in love with a woman to create change in your own life. Any which way it happens for you is good.)

10

Start With Yourself

'Fear, to a great extent, is born of a story we tell ourselves, and so I chose to tell myself a different story from the one women are told. I decided I was safe. I was strong. I was brave. Nothing could vanquish me.' Cheryl Strayed, Wild

I've lost count of the number of times I've heard the phrase 'It's business' during my working life. And by that people mean 'This isn't personal. Don't get emotional.' Try telling that to someone who's got three kids to support and has just been sacked.

Work is personal. Really personal. Through it, we can create a sense of progress, accomplishment and community. It fuels our self-esteem, happiness and confidence.

The kinds of feelings that anyone who says, 'It's business' means are the 'messy', 'feminine' ones, like sadness or fear. Start crying in a business meeting and your card will be marked. 'Weak' emotions have no place in alpha culture.

But the irony is that the whole thing is deeply emotional: wanting to smash the competition and be top dog isn't exactly unfeeling, is it?

For me, starting to work like a woman was all about putting

more feeling into work – not less – by learning to allow a whole spectrum of feelings to come into play.

To get you to the point where I started to do that would mean talking you through every cough and spit of my first decade in business, including my holidays to my favourite Greek island and Kevin the canary dying.

I won't.

Suffice to say, I continued to work how I'd always worked for many years after starting the agency. Falling in love with a woman might have shifted something fundamental in me but it didn't transform me overnight into a whole new person at work.

Professionally, for a long time, I was pretty much the same old Mary and continued to follow the rules I'd been taught by alpha culture: I was a good negotiator, focused on the bottom line and fiercely ambitious. All of which served me well.

It was only when I unexpectedly launched a whole new career that I started on the journey that would eventually lead me to finding a new way to work.

When Graham left the business following our divorce, Peter Cross joined me at the agency as managing director and soon became my closest professional confidant and dear friend. For the next decade, we worked to build a business with global brands like Louis Vuitton, Acne and Mercedes. The Portas team grew to about forty people and it was a fun, creative and exciting time.

Then, in 2006, I was approached by the venerable TV producer Pat Llewellyn, who'd seen me appear as a guest on an afternoon TV show and thought I'd be good doing more on screen. She signed me up to present a show that featured me going into small struggling retail businesses and applying my ideas and experience to turn them around. It's worth pointing out that I was forty-six when I started this new career, so give yourself a talking-to the next time you tell yourself you're too old to get the job/fall in love/move home. You are not!

Mary Queen of Shops first aired on the BBC in 2007 and I went on to make two more series – and meet the most wonderful cast of characters. People like Denny and Dazzle, whose furniture shop in Kingston-upon-Thames looked like a dodgy YMCA meets Russian swinging party when I got there. I don't think they knew what had hit them when I arrived.

Denny and Dazzle were a unique combination and I couldn't help but like them. They were good, talented people, who'd never had any real business guidance. They were making many mistakes and losing a lot of money. Advising them gave me a huge sense of satisfaction. As did seeing them flourish and regain their confidence as I worked with them.

I connected with everyone I worked with. Well, almost. The less said about Angela-the-baker-who-eventually-barricaded-herself-in-her-shop-and-refused-to-let-me-in the better. I never felt like I was making a TV show. This was personal: I was advising people on how to protect their livelihoods and their sense of self-worth. All those I worked with were grappling with a sense of failure because their business was failing, and I helped them replace that with hope. It was really rewarding to do so.

In 2009, the format was tweaked and, instead of going into privately owned shops, I tackled charity retail. So many of these shops look and feel down at heel. They often seem unloved, and people complain there are too many of them on high streets. But the core of charity shops is about people giving back: they're about community, staffed mainly by local volunteers, and raise money for vital causes. They should be a treasured part of any high street.

I thought that transforming charity shops into beautiful spaces people wanted to shop in could transform their image – and fortunes. People would donate better stuff, there would be new volunteers and more money would be raised for important causes.

I thought a lot about it and felt really committed to the project. What I hadn't expected, though, was to meet a generation of women who profoundly changed me.

Arriving in the Orpington branch of Save the Children, I found many of the volunteers were older women, the kind of women who'd disappeared from my life after my parents died. Stuck among the china figurines and tatty paperbacks were women with a deep sense of duty and social conscience, women who wanted to give up their time to help those less fortunate than themselves.

It was a world away from the individualistic sphere of work I was used to. Those women didn't give a toss about status and power – as I found out early on when I asked one to change the outfit on a mannequin. 'Do it yourself,' she said, to the TV presenter/CEO/one 'in charge'.

I was speechless. Then I laughed.

On the final day of filming, the volunteers lined up to say goodbye and I felt truly sad that I wouldn't see them again. There was Brenda, smiling broadly at me alongside the octogenarian 'toy twins', who turned up every single day, come rain, snow or shine. I knew then that I just couldn't leave them all behind, pack up another piece of work well done. Because what had struck me most while working with them was this: what was *I* giving back?

The thought stayed with me as the show aired and the

overhaul of the Orpington shop proved a great success. It went from being one of Save the Children's worst-performing stores to one of its top ten. Soon, I approached the charity – headed by two great women, Tanya Steele and Jayne Cartwright – to partner with me on expanding the concept.

We opened the first Mary's Living & Giving charity shop in 2009. Today there are twenty-five stores, which have raised more than £12 million for some of our most disadvantaged children. And while I'm delighted this money has supported such vital work, I'm no selfless do-gooder. Starting to give back taught me one very important lesson: you get as much, if not more, in return for what you give.

I don't know whether to cry or be sick.

I'm staring at a headline in one of Britain's biggest newspapers. It reads: 'Mary the Queen of Flops'. Yet another article attacking me publicly.

Every time my face is on a page under yet another crappy headline, I want to bury myself a bit more. But I can't. I have a business to run, employees and, of course, a family to look after. People depend on me and I have to keep going however much this hurts my pride. I try to get angry when I'm attacked. But mostly I just feel incredibly hurt.

It started in 2011 when the government asked me to look at issues affecting Britain's high streets and deliver a report on safeguarding them for the future. I desperately wanted to do this piece of work because, having travelled the length and breadth of the country while filming my TV series, I'd seen up close what was happening in many town centres. They were in trouble.

The reality was harsh. Boarded-up grocers, and fashion shops whose clients had deserted them in favour of out-of-town shopping centres or online retail, an explosion of pound and betting shops, libraries and community centres closing down, kids hanging around on street corners. It had made me understand that I could do nothing to help people whose businesses were dying if the town around them was dying too. They were fighting a losing battle.

I didn't exactly have the time for extra work when I was asked to do the high-street report. By now, in addition to running the agency and TV work, I also had a fashion line, wrote a newspaper column and gave lectures. I barely found a moment to brush my teeth each morning.

But looking at what could be done to reverse the tide of decline was about protecting whole communities: a thriving high street is a focal point for people to gather and a place that provides jobs and other key services in addition to retail. It is the heartbeat of most communities. It goes way beyond politics. This was a vital piece of work that I had to do.

And, just like that, I naively went sailing into a perfect storm.

This project was political – a complex game of competing interests: national and local politicians who set business rates and created legislation; property owners who earned income from renting out retail spaces; shopkeepers; community groups and the public.

Everyone wanted a say.

For the next year, I spent at least one day a week travelling the UK to meet people and hear their ideas, talk about the problems and discover what solutions there might be.

When the report was finally published, it contained twenty-eight recommendations, including the setting up of 'Town Teams' to manage high streets, cutting through unnecessary red tape and implementing free parking schemes to encourage more footfall.

I also suggested testing the ideas in pilot projects, and soon £1.2 million of initial funding had been allocated for a dozen towns to do this. I was asked to put my name to the whole thing and agreed. I wanted to see the ideas tested and learn the lessons that might be adopted on a bigger scale.

But we should all – and this is a really key lesson I learned – play to our strengths.

I should have been happy with the work I'd done in analysing the state of the high street, walked away knowing I'd contributed to an important issue and left someone else to guide the project through choppy political waters.

I didn't because I felt committed to it.

But the project had critical faults from day one. The money was enough to test ideas. It was there to help us start to get a deeper understanding of the needs of each town and act as a foundation for further work, but nowhere near sufficient to reinvent one high street – let alone twelve.

There was some truly innovative thinking happening at grass roots in the towns, from farmers' markets to pop-up shops, the renovation of buildings and the development of 'digital high streets' – websites and apps that give vital information on local businesses. The number of pilot towns was ultimately extended, and so much inspiring, committed work came out of them, from Rotherham to Ashford, Loughborough to London.

But at a higher level, the whole thing became a political bun fight, more about power-playing and one-upmanship than collaborative pulling together for the greater good. There were, of course, some great people involved, but also many others with louder voices who were there to knock their opponents and drive their own agenda.

I should have felt at home. I was used to all that power-playing in the working world. But I just found it depressing in that context.

Soon newspaper stories started to appear detailing all the 'failures' of the high-street pilots as the chorus of disapproval grew louder. This was the government's project more than mine: ministers made key decisions while I was an adviser. But my name was on every headline because I was the figurehead.

Over the next year, the problems and criticisms kept coming: shops were closing in Portas Pilot Towns and the pilot money was not being well spent. The project had never been about short-term figures on shop closures, though. My ideas were about the kind of regeneration that would take years – but all that got lost.

My relationship with Peter, who had practically worked full-time with me on the pilots, was put under a lot of stress. We bickered, we fought and, after so many successes and nearly ten years together, the most significant working relationship I had fell apart as he left the agency.

I continued with a very heavy heart. The core of my business was strong because the agency continued to deliver good work, but it was a lonely, soul-destroying time.

And, deep inside, the sense of wanting to give back sparked by my time in the charity shops collided with the most bruising experience of combative working I'd ever had.

I knew I had to take some time to pull back and think, to learn what I could from all these experiences. Now Peter had gone, I also had to work out a new future for me as well as my business.

But what? I had no idea.

*

In the week Melanie gave birth to our son Horatio in September 2012, Mylo left our family home to start university. Two huge moments of change. But I hardly had time to let those events settle inside me because I was back on TV within weeks.

This time, I was making a series in which I went head to head with chef Gordon Ramsay as we ran a hotel: him in charge of kitchen and restaurant, me acting as general manager of the rest.

Celebrities would come in to work for us, as well as fourteen unemployed young people on work experience, two of whom would get a job at the end of the series – one with Gordon and one with me. The programme would also raise money for youth unemployment charities. Gordon and I would compete to see who could earn the most money.

It's no exaggeration to say that I wanted to stick my head in a blender almost the moment the whole thing began.

It was excruciating.

Gordon Ramsay has made a name for himself by being big, loud and the most alpha in the room. I knew I was going to have to bring all my alpha game to the show – and more – if I was going to stand up against him and 'win'.

So I did.

But instead of relishing the challenge as I once had, I found it demoralizing, soul-destroying and deeply unfulfilling. Marching around, trying to be the big I-am felt fake.

My alpha streak is, of course, a part of me and had also served me well during my career. But my TV work on *Queen of Shops* had tapped into another side of me. It was about more than swinging my balls. It was about emotionally connecting with people, and that was what I enjoyed. Not head-butting with Gordon Ramsay.

The show was broadcast live for five nights, and I'd get home to find Melanie on the sofa with the baby and a sad look on her face. Her expression said it all: what on earth are you doing?

By the end of filming, I felt as if I'd reached my lowest ebb. After the high-street pilots, the split with Peter and now this, I realized I was lost in a way I never had been before. And, for perhaps the first time in my adult life, strong, capable Mary Portas didn't have an answer.

By a lot of people's standards, I was successful: I'd built the agency, had other strands to my business life, and my TV profile had made me a bit 'famous'. But was it all bringing me joy? We live in a world that idolizes celebrity but it didn't feel that great to me.

In the months that followed, I couldn't shake the feeling that somehow I had to make radical changes to my life and I thought more than I ever had before about how I was living it.

And what I gradually realized was that I'd spent my life since my parents died outrunning my grief, making myself so busy at work – and trying to provide financial security for myself and those I loved – that I didn't have to stop and feel the deep sense of loss because I never wanted to feel that vulnerable again.

I'd become very strong, a provider, and chased the things that alpha culture had said would make me safe: money, success and power. And I *was* safe – financially at least. I just wasn't happy deep in my soul.

I believe now that I had been preparing for that crisis point. My instinct had told me it was coming. In the years leading up to that moment, I'd been doing a lot of reading: everything from philosophy and science to spiritual thinkers: Aristotle and Socrates, Pema Chödrön, Vandana Shiva and Eckhart Tolle. Not having been to university, I had invested time at home in self-learning, and I drank it all in. I was looking for answers and ideas on how to make a really fundamental change in my working life before I even understood that I had to make it.

Some people, of course, do this kind of searching a lot earlier in life than I did. But now at fifty-two, well into middle age, I finally had a period of looking back at how I had lived, and forward to how I wanted to live the next stage of my life. I also had the luxury of having made enough money to step back from the day-to-day grind and take stock.

And the more I thought about it, the more I realized that while I was now softer, less guarded, less tough, and far more vulnerable in my personal life, I was still working in the way I had been taught: autonomous, single-minded and driven by the bottom line.

If I was truly honest, while I loved the clients I'd worked with for years and bits of what I did, I also didn't love much of what I had created at the agency – even though the money was coming in. It wasn't enough any more.

Using my mind creatively to help people and businesses effect change – and give something back to the greater good – brought me joy.

But how on earth could I change the way I worked? This was how I'd done it for more than twenty years. I was good at it. I was at the top of the pile in many ways.

To answer that question, I started to write down feelings and ideas, trying desperately to articulate what was going on inside me. I kept an orange notebook by my bed and would scribble down quotes that inspired me, as well as thoughts about what I enjoyed and what I felt uneasy with.

Here's an example:

- Things I love: working with bright people; helping them succeed; solving business problems; setting goals; laughing; being mischievous; feeling free; feeling energized by great projects
- Things I care about: my family; my employees; fighting for the underdog and underprivileged; the environment; my charity shops
- Things I'm good at: having a vision; leading instinctively; inspiring people
- Things I'm not good at: detail; working alone; spreadsheets; networking; politics
- Things I need to do: be responsible for three children; pay the mortgage; look after my staff; be fit and healthy
- Things I don't want to do: work with people who are boring, egotistical or treat me well but not my team; meetings over two hours; work past 6 p.m.; play a political game; long hours and weekend work

The book was a mass of ideas, thoughts and inspiration. But bit by bit as I filled it, I saw there was one central theme: control.

Now, many of us want to control our lives to make them safe. But I'd been maxing out on it: in rigid control of mine since the chaos created by my parents' deaths.

Meeting Melanie had made me give up control personally in many ways because it forced me to live differently. And while my family and friends had been accepting, I'd also had to be out and proud about the woman I loved to the world at large because I had a public profile. The reaction of that world is something you can never control so I'd had to accept that I couldn't. And it had taught me that I could not only survive but thrive when I did.

And yet, at work, my life was still dominated by control: trying to ensure there were concrete outcomes and income. It wasn't making me happy any more.

The agency was successful and profitable, though. Was I really going to risk all that?

For the next year, I simply gave all these thoughts space. I sat with them. I gave them oxygen. I read. I meditated. I listened, I wrote. And I gave it time.

I slowly realized that what I really wanted to do was work in a way that reflected all of who I was and what I believed in, a way that not only played to my strengths but those of the people around me.

I wanted to allow everyone in my business to be true to what we did well and work with clients for the love of it – not just the profit. My intuition told me that working this way would bring true rewards: financial, emotional and professional.

And I somehow understood that the way to make this happen was by blending the 'work' Mary with the 'private' Mary and have my true self, my values and characteristics reflected in the way I worked. That meant tapping into my most feminine qualities – empathy, vulnerability, intuition and resilience – instead of suppressing them to fit into the alpha mould. It was time to work as I really was.

But how would I do that?

11

If It Ain't Broke, Why Fix It?

Jorkin: 'Why don't you sell out while the going's good? You'll never get a better offer. It's the age of the machine, and the factory, and the vested interests. We small traders are ancient history, Mr Fezziwig.'

Fezziwig: 'It's not just for money alone that one spends a lifetime building up a business ... It's to preserve a way of life that one knew and loved. No, I can't see my way to selling out to the new vested interests, Mr Jorkin. I'll have to be loyal to the old ways and die out with them if needs must.'
Charles Dickens, A Christmas Carol

I've put this quote in for my pal Penny, who calls me Fezziwig Portas. It always makes me laugh. We share many moments chatting together about ideas on how to play our part in making the world a better place. (Usually over a couple of bottles of wine.)

And, happily, more and more businesses are doing the same: thinking about how to do their bit to improve the way they work and we live – from looking at their environmental impact or supply chain to working with the wider community.

I'd love to be around in fifty years to see what effect it's all had.

Getting more women to the top is also on the list of necessary changes, and a key argument is that diversity is good for the bottom line.

But should making work more fair and inclusive really just be a question of opening up opportunities for making more money? Isn't it just the right thing to do in a world that has changed so much?

I'm in no way implying that 'business' and 'profit' are negatives of course. Not all companies are reckless profiteers who mindlessly destroy the environment or capitalize on the misery of their disenfranchised workers. (Although, sadly, there are too many of those idiots out there.)

I certainly enjoy the basic principle of working to make money and realizing personal and collective potential. It is one of the things that drive me. I started work with very little and have enjoyed building a business and making myself financially secure.

But should the maximization of profit be the only measure of success?

There are plenty of people – including chief executives and company directors – who don't believe it is, and companies can now also be ranked on the happiness of their workers. So can countries, as the idea of national happiness – instead of just the numbers involved in GDP – takes hold as a way to grade a nation's prosperity.

But even if new ideas are starting to gain momentum, the old one that financial success – or failure – is the key assessment of a business still retains an iron grip.

And what's the point of a nation, a company or a person being financially wealthy but miserable as sin? If money is the sole motivator for making work more equitable, aren't we just using the same old alpha mindset to justify the measures being put in place?

Money is certainly important. It pays wages and bills, drives national and global economies. But making the most possible money can also come at a huge cost – socially and environmentally. Yet we still celebrate it.

Take *The Apprentice*: the most high-profile business TV show on UK telly is driven by the ethos of maximizing profit.

Never mind the backbiting seen during the boardroom firings that are a dog-eat-dog blame fest overseen by Lord Sugar. Or the power-playing apparent in the Final Five 'interviews' – in which contestants are mauled by a grand-standing panel of 'experts'. Week in, week out, a team can mess the whole thing up and behave like buffoons but still win if they make the most money.

And while Lord Sugar inevitably saves the day and lets common sense triumph by stopping someone who's good at making money but impossible to work with winning the title, the focus of the show still comes down to who makes the most profit each week. And this prioritizing of short-term profit over any other consideration reflects much of our wider working culture.

I know *The Apprentice* is entertainment TV but it pays little attention to a host of other vital business skills, like leadership, teambuilding and not being a total ****** to name a few. It is the show that gave the world Katie Hopkins, after all.

(Just for the record, if *The Apprentice* does end up on the TV in my house when my kids are home, I usually spend most of it screaming: 'You're all fired because you're all crap.')

But it wasn't always this way.

For a long time, many businesses embraced a wider commitment to community and society. Just look at the Quakers who built British institutions like Rowntrees and Cadbury, Lloyds Bank and Clarks shoes at the same time as housing their workers, and giving them pensions and access to medical care. But in the 1970s the mindset shifted after influential economists argued that the primary function of any business was to maximize shareholder value – otherwise known as making the most money.

Soon Margaret Thatcher had taken power on one side of the Atlantic and Ronald Reagan on the other. The idea of maximizing profits took hold. And CEOs had an increasingly vested interest in maximizing shareholder value as stock options became a common perk.

The rise in CEO pay is quite frankly jaw-dropping. The average US CEO now makes 271 times what the average worker does. In 1989, it was fifty-nine times and in 1965 a mere twenty. In the UK, a CEO makes £129 for every pound the average employee makes. In 1987, it was £45. You can see how things have spiralled out of control. Even some of those running public bodies and not-for-profit organizations are on salaries that would make most British workers gasp.

How can these people look themselves in the eye and justify this kind of money? It's sheer greed.

Of course there are specific challenges for companies that are answerable to shareholders who rely on a good stock price for their income. I have ultimate control over my business because I own it.

But a shift is happening even in big businesses as influential leaders begin to call for change.

And if companies are embracing this kind of social responsibility, we also need to do our bit. As consumers, we demand fast fashion that's often made cheaply by women and children in lower-income countries. We want food prices to be as low as possible, regardless of economic impact, animal welfare and environmental issues. We order taxis or deliveries at the cheapest possible price – with people on often unstable and low-paid zero-hours contracts providing the services.

In many instances, alpha culture has put maximizing profits at its heart. But we're often the ones keeping it there.

If moral imperatives aren't your thing, here's another key driver for changing the way we work: Millennials and Generation Z.

As Generation Z are starting to work, Millennials are now already well into their careers and will make up three-quarters of the global workforce by 2025. But while they're often portrayed – in the media at least – as free spirits who want to acquire multiple skills across a varied career path (or, depending on which newspaper you're reading, feckless opportunists with little loyalty and a bad phone habit), I've found that Millennials are none of the above, having employed many of them.

They are committed, energetic, and often want to make the world a better place. They're also much more like the rest of us than we're often led to believe.

Research shows that Millennials share a lot of common ground with older employees, including the desire for decent pay and flexible working, and aversion to excessive overtime.

In fact, if anything, older workers are the takers because they focus on pay, development and control over their work, while Millennials place greater importance on team cohesion, supervisor support and flexibility.

Despite the similarities, though, we know that younger workers are prepared to leave jobs if they don't feel they're getting what they need from them. I don't blame them. I got to exactly that point myself. Many women do. But it's an increasing problem for businesses that are competing to recruit and retain talent.

Younger workers are not less 'loyal' or difficult to please. Like all of us, they see work as a financial exchange. It's just that they want it to be part of a whole life, and there's less reason than there used to be for them to stick with jobs that don't either pay well or satisfy other aspirations.

Jobs for life are mostly a thing of the past. The portfolio career has been embraced and, in an economically unstable world with little promise of financial security, why stick around if your job isn't giving you what you want from it? Alpha culture survived on financial reward and linear advancement for a long time but it's no longer enough.

And, luckily for women, what Millennials want from work is fundamentally what we have been wanting, too, for a long time – more flexibility and a better balance between work and family life. The younger generation might well be the catalyst to the kind of change we've wanted for years but been denied.

And it's imperative that we find a way to work that better reflects all that we want from work. Because it's not just a pay cheque.

12

Embracing Uncertainty

'Nothing ever goes away, until it has taught us what we need to know.' Pema Chödrön, When Things Fall Apart: Heart Advice for Difficult Times

As I grappled with the deep feeling of uncertainty about the way I was working, I reverted to type and went back to what was familiar.

Throughout 2013, I got in consultants, talked to head hunters and looked at employing people with the 'right' CVs. I also paid for lots of expensive lunches with people I hoped would give me good advice.

'You need a total c***,' one business friend, who had sold his company for millions, told me. 'Someone who'll come in and deliver on the numbers.'

And I swear my first thought was: That *is* what I need. Where can I find one? And aren't total c***s very expensive?

Why? Because change is really hard – even if you've decided to embrace it – and however much I'd connected with the theme addressed by many of the thinkers I'd read, about how to build a meaningful, authentic life, it was hard to start letting go of all I'd been taught by alpha culture. Rational, fact-based alpha culture tells us that meaning is found in power and money and stuff, that the big house, status and kudos mean 'success'.

So, to be honest, I didn't even know how to start talking about the idea that there might be a different path to follow. It excited me but I was also worried it would sound a bit too much like new-age thinking – which has no place at work. Mention anything remotely emotional or spiritual within a hundred feet of most offices and people turn pale. And even if you work in an industry in which talking about your lunch-time yoga class or new mindfulness technique is acceptable, the zen is often shed as soon as you step into a meeting and straight back into aggressive, competitive alpha mode.

But in addition to the thinkers and philosophers, I also read about other businesses that had connected their deep values with their commercial enterprise, and this encouraged me.

And the more I thought about it, the more I saw that I wasn't going to be sitting there in knitted muesli socks preaching about renouncing all worldly goods. What I wanted was to be open about my desire to integrate practical, material ambition with being my whole, authentic self and working in a way that reflected it.

It was time to let go of the fear and start creating change.

But being the leader of a business who wants to take it in a completely different direction felt lonely, and I knew I needed support. Everyone in my working world was on my payroll and I needed someone with no financial interest in what I wanted to do. I needed a friend.

I found one in Neil Rodford, CEO of the James Grant Group – a big talent agency that I was signed up to because of my TV work.

I'd always liked Neil, felt comfortable in his company; and

mentioned to him over lunch one day that I was finding it hard always to be the one in charge, the decision-maker, when I wasn't yet sure of exactly where I wanted to go.

'I'll help,' he said.

And he did. For the next year, Neil met with me regularly to talk, sat down with my senior staff and guided us through an exciting, but tough, process of change, looking at what I wanted to achieve and how we might go about making it happen. He's a busy man, with a demanding job of his own, and did all this without asking for anything in return.

The only thing he said he wanted when we talked it over during that first lunch was a thank-you some day.

So here it is: thank you, Neil, for being wise, kind and incredibly generous with your time. You're a great man.

My home education had taught me that if I wanted my external working world to shift, I had first to work on me. And top of the list was relinquishing some of the control I'd cultivated through being a leader.

Titles are key in alpha culture because we're a nation obsessed with being named 'managers' and the status that confers. I, too, was definitely invested in being recognized as the leader of my business with the title CEO.

But as I looked back on my life as an entrepreneur, and was really honest for perhaps the first time about who I was, I realized that heading up the agency as number-one honcho was not what I should be doing, or the best use of me.

By now the agency had more than fifty staff, consulting and creating campaigns for many global brands. I had also built parallel careers and my life was extraordinarily full.

But sustaining it, growing it and, most of all, controlling it was exhausting. The linear hierarchy I'd built at the agency had me at the top signing off most decisions, and that had to change. I was a fairly good leader but my true skill lay in developing the creative solutions. So, first off, I let go of the need to be the head of Portas. It was neither bringing me joy nor making business sense.

I became the Portas Agency's chief creative officer. There to lead, create and provide vision but leaving much of the practical, daily steering of the business in other hands.

The second step was finally allowing my intuition to drive my business decisions as well as my creative ones. I'd always used intuition to come up with ideas but rarely to make 'rational' business decisions. True happiness and progress, though, had only ever come for me when I had connected with my inner self and instinct.

Now I was going to use that powerful instinct to put people in place who I believed would be the best for my business – and instead of looking outside the agency to find them, I was going to look inward.

I'd fallen into a classic trap: imposter syndrome. I'd been so busy thinking that people who were external to the business had the answers because they were so sure of themselves, convinced that they knew better, that I hadn't seen we actually already had them inside the company.

Caireen Wackett had worked for me for ten years and been promoted to managing director, reporting to the CEO during that time. She was talented, driven, incredibly hard-working and fiercely intelligent. She'd never been in total day-to-day charge of a business but I knew she'd be the perfect person for the job because she'd risen to every promotional challenge she'd been set while working for me. She was also loyal and I knew I could completely trust her.

On the board with her would be finance director Mark

Nicholson, who had worked with me for years, and Richard Danks, who'd risen through the ranks to become brand director.

Caireen, Mark and Richard all had immense talent. We shared common values and that, to me, was absolutely central to success. Together we aspired to become the best agency doing the best work with the best people.

This core business goal would become the foundation of everything that followed. And if your purpose is shared, that energy lights you up and together you become a light that others want to follow.

So, I've started to let go of control and the new board is in place. What next?

We began by creating a new business model for our clients that could adapt in a free-flowing way to the ever-changing needs of today's consumers. We needed to be nimble and innovative in advising retailers on how to connect to the shifting cultural zeitgeist of how people were living and consuming.

This new approach required a fair bit of investment in people and place. I've lost count of the number of offices I've been to where the work on global, glamorous brands is done by people working in crappy offices with a view of a dual carriageway.

We found new, light, open-plan office premises in Bloomsbury, a 'village' in London full of history, cafés and shops. We wanted to connect with the community by using local businesses and create a space in which Portas people wanted to be – as well as work – so desk space was combined with eating and seating areas. Three years on, I still have a smile on my face every time I walk through the front door.

Then, we looked at the team we knew were crucial to our new Portas model and raised some salaries to acknowledge that they were important to us as well as the business. We also created a new tier of middle management to solve a disconnect between the people at the top and those further down the business. Some were promoted into it and others were hired.

We'd also fallen into another common trap: people were doing many jobs instead of the one they were best at and loved. Creatives were worrying about logistics; directors were bogged down in HR issues. We created new departments to split work into clearly defined areas and allow people to focus on what they were best at.

And for those coming into the company, our HR brief was redrawn. Alongside the practicalities of qualifications and experience, we started to ask what potential employees were like as people. Were they bright? Were they happy? Would we want to sit across from them at a dinner table? Skills alone were not enough. We wanted positive, participative people working with us.

Instead of controlling outcomes, we would place the best work as our guiding principle, underpinned with a set of core values, and leave people to get on with their jobs.

So, for instance, I handed over full control of my diary to my treasured assistant Abi as well as Caireen, Richard and Mark. When they needed me in the office, they put it in the diary. I didn't micro-manage decisions any more. They made them, and only pulled me into the process when they felt I needed to be involved.

For me, it felt very freeing not to have to be 'in charge' of everything all the time.

But perhaps the most important change we made was in

how we approached finances. Not wanting to be strait-jacketed by profit goals any more, we sat down to look objectively at how we could responsibly start again.

We had to pay salaries and meet our financial obligations for the next year because, while we were open to change, we also had a moral obligation to make sure that the business was safe. But our core financial obligations were the only thing we structured. The rest was up for grabs. We were in a place of uncertainty. And, as strange as it might sound, it felt great. Liberating, even.

Rather than create numbers from the top down and strive to meet them, we looked realistically at what sort of agency we wanted to be and where we wanted to take the business, built the numbers from the bottom up, set costs against them and accepted that our profit for the next year would probably be zero.

Yes. Zero. After fifteen years of constantly making a healthy profit, we were starting again at profit neutral. (Otherwise known as blowing alpha culture's golden rule out of the water.) Because while financial metrics are a good guide to where you should be heading, a business needs to work to more than just numbers.

Metrics can't capture the joining together of a team of people to create the best work. They don't take into account the messy thing that is life either – in which people unexpectedly need time off or projects don't come together.

I had been working too rigidly towards numbers for a long time, despite the creativity at the heart of what my business did. So, metrics would be used in combination with openness to fluidity and change – even financial change.

There are so many things that can affect the way you work or the market you're working in. We had to learn to adapt to the unexpected and, instead of seeing it as a negative, use it to create something positive.

What we did certainly needed courage. Moving away from the linear path to success and embracing uncertainty can be uncomfortable. And while we knew we could sustain this new financial structure short-term, we didn't yet have the business to do so for ever.

But we felt confident in taking a leap of faith because we believed this level of support would free people to do their best work. And this, in turn, would attract more work.

And we were right.

In the years since then, we've hit our numbers almost all the time. But there's also been enough flexibility to allow us to adjust financial targets on the occasions that we couldn't. These things happen. But instead of sticking to an unrealistic figure, we now look at why we got it wrong and whether we can do anything to avoid that again.

But let's be clear on one thing: uncertainty is not the same as the kind of risk that alpha culture certainly embraces. From the oil workers on the rig who wanted to 'prove' their bravery until they found a different way to work, to the mind-boggling chances that were taken in the money markets before the global crash, risk is a key way to prove machismo.

Uncertainty is different. It's about making a plan, doing all you can to enact it based on skills, knowledge and experience, working with a value system to guide you while at the same time accepting that you cannot completely control the outcome.

It's about responsiveness and flexibility, trusting your business to change and flow, sensing that and responding to it as it happens, instead of rigidity and control.

And for me, these are deeply feminine skills that women have been learning for millennia. We are carers, and that's what the job is all about: adapting to uncertainty and responding flexibly. Whether it's working out what to do if the baby won't sleep, or the toddler gets tonsillitis, or the elderly parent won't change the habits of a lifetime, the list is endless.

The world is changing, social codes are falling away and cracks are appearing in the old way of doing things. Starting to work like a woman is about abandoning the codes we have traditionally worked to for the very new territory of uncertainty.

There is a poem painted on the wall near the front door of my agency. It's the first thing people see when they walk in and I first heard it when I had just won an audition to RADA aged eighteen.

I'd always wanted to train as an actress. It was my true passion and I should have been ecstatic. But instead, having just lost Mum, I was feeling so vulnerable and scared that I went to see my drama teacher to tell him I couldn't do it.

That afternoon, he read me a poem by Christopher Logue:

> *Come to the edge.*
> *We might fall.*
> *Come to the edge.*
> *It's too high.*
> *COME TO THE EDGE!*
> *And they came,*
> *And he pushed,*
> *And they flew.*

So I did. I went to the audition and got a place. Then life took over so I didn't go to RADA and went out to work instead. But since then I've flown in other ways because I learned young to take a leap into uncertainty.

Now is the time for business to learn this vital lesson too.

13

Starting From the Top Down

'A strong woman understands that the gifts such as logic, decisiveness and strength are just as feminine as intuition and emotional connection. She values and uses all her gifts.'
Nancy Rathburn

The Design & Art Direction Festival is devoted to all things creative, full of bright people with bright ideas. And, judging from the latest exhibition, the move towards a more diverse world is inevitable. Even white, middle-aged, middle-class men attending the event – the ones with most to lose – agreed that it was time for things to change.

Diversity right now is a hot topic – a business buzzword – because it's pretty much accepted that men dominate the top of work and something has to give. Most large businesses are working on bringing more women – and anyone else who is under-represented – into their business and understanding how they think.

It's simple, really: a diverse group of people provide different perspectives, and harnessing their individuality as they work together offers more powerful possibilities than employing a group of people with a more similar mindset.

Jaguar Land Rover faced a huge challenge in recruiting

more women because engineering has historically been a very male industry, and Jaguar Land Rover is the kind of company people stay with for years. So while they wanted to make their business more equal when it came to male and female employees, they knew they needed to start from the 'bottom' up. In 2012, Jaguar Land Rover began targeting young women to recruit as engineering apprentices by offering them the chance to spend a week with the company, seeing how it worked.

It was a great success.

The company's current apprentice and graduate intake is now fifty:fifty. In years to come, as those young women move up through the business, its engineering workforce will be far more equal.

Good on you, Jaguar Land Rover, for thinking creatively about doing your bit to tackle issues of gender diversity in the workforce.

Elsewhere, the drive to get more women into UK boardrooms has also begun to work. Companies like Sky have significantly increased their numbers of women leaders and others, like Goldman Sachs, are working to empower women at grass-roots level by supporting female entrepreneurs in fifty-six countries.

I applaud all this. It's vital work. But I don't believe focusing on numbers is enough, and even formalizing them via quotas won't be either. We also have to believe in changing the culture in which we work and start to create one that values and rewards long-suppressed but vital feminine characteristics and viewpoints. This is what will create a more balanced way of working that enables women to reach the top.

In my business, that has meant tapping into my deepest

truth about who I am as a woman, bringing my full self to work and creating a new culture based on those values. And I think other small businesses like mine could have a key advantage over the big ones in creating a similar culture shift.

Big business is certainly talking about this but I'm not yet convinced that always goes deeper than top-line statistics. Changing the culture of a big organization is like turning around a tanker: it's heavy work and takes a long time.

To create real change, you've got to put some soul into it. This is what the best businesses need. And when I say 'soul', I don't mean accountancy firms offering meditation classes, or retailing coming up with such clever packaging it looks as if their eggs were hatched on a Devon smallholding rather than battery-farmed on the outskirts of Clacton.

Soul, for me, is about a shared personal connection within your organization that allows everyone to achieve their individual and collective potential. And, because of their size, this might well be easier to inject into smaller businesses that have a head start on personal connection in comparison to massive corporations.

The good news is that almost half of us in the UK don't work for the big hitters. For every GlaxoSmithKline there are a hundred companies like mine, employing everyone from plumbers to bookkeepers, architects to sound engineers.

These smaller companies may therefore be crucial to changing the way we work, and while they certainly face challenges – namely, that they don't have either the money or time needed to create headline-grabbing leadership programmes and diversity initiatives – what they do have are leaders who can be far more closely connected with staff at all levels, and the ability to be more nimble.

So if all our smaller businesses got stuck into this, I believe we could see quite remarkable – and rapid – change.

It's entirely possible. You've just got to believe in what you're doing. And so must your staff.

In late 2008, doctors at the Birmingham Children's Hospital revealed serious misgivings about care, safety measures and unresponsive senior management that together were putting patients at risk. A government inquiry was launched. Something was clearly very wrong with both the working environment and the culture it was rooted in.

Sarah-Jane Marsh was BCH's chief operating officer at the time and the board of directors asked her to step in as interim chief executive while they looked for a permanent replacement. But after struggling to find one, the board realized a new approach was needed. The chair asked Sarah-Jane, who was thirty-two at the time, to take on the job. It was a huge task: she had relatively little board experience and would be responsible for 2700 employees, as well as patients.

Now, every culture change is different. BCH didn't need to get more women into their workforce because 83 per cent were female. Instead, it was about putting more female values at the heart of a failing institution as a way to heal it.

Sarah-Jane started with urgent practical tasks, like funding and staffing levels. But then, instead of going the classic route of sitting in her office, looking at the data, writing up lots of well-meaning culture documents and getting other people to do the on-the-ground work, she did something unusual. Sarah-Jane got herself a video camera and started talking to staff. She wanted to know what values they believed were at the heart of the organization that employed them.

Over the next two years, Sarah-Jane carried on talking to staff about these values: compassion, courage, trust, commitment and respect. Then she took the talking and used it to enable people to enact cultural change on a wider level because, just like I do, Sarah-Jane believes that work isn't just a numbers game.

The NHS might be a vocation for many of those working in it but I don't think many people in any job do it just for the pay packet. It's about everything from meaning and community to purpose, a sense of progression and not getting stuck on the sofa watching reruns of *Real Housewives* all day.

At BCH, Sarah-Jane started to transform the culture by rooting each working day in the core values her staff had told her about. They were referenced everywhere from appraisals to staff events and used as tools to aid decision-making: did a proposed action reflect BCH's core values? Even junior team members were now able to feed into decisions made by more senior staff – often rare in the classically alpha environment of medicine, with its adherence to rigid hierarchy – by referring to the values.

Voices from all staffing levels were heard and this was key to creating the idea of 'team BCH' – another crucial plank in enabling an organization filled with individuals to transform into a group of people pulling together to do their best work.

The final strand to culture change at BCH was to admit failures and use the lessons learned to improve. Instead of stonewalling criticism and refusing to face up to errors, Sarah-Jane wanted to serve patients' best interests by listening to and acting on what they said had gone wrong.

In 2017 BCH became the first children's hospital of its kind in the UK to be rated outstanding by inspectors from the Care Quality Commission. In just eight years, this large organization had undergone profound cultural change.

Sarah-Jane's masterstroke was to understand that, while she had to lead from the front, her job was also to create the conditions in which thousands of people felt their viewpoints were heard, then pulled together and created radical change.

And I believe she achieved this by putting feminine values, like flexibility and collaboration, at the heart of her organization, as well as allowing herself to be led by her instinct about what would work to create change.

Imagine if there were more people like Sarah-Jane leading the thousands of small and medium-sized businesses that are currently operating in the UK right now. We'd all be working like women – and benefiting hugely from it – before we knew it.

As well as embracing uncertainty and allowing intuition to drive my business – and creative – decisions, there were other characteristics that I valued as a woman and wanted to weave into the way I – and my company – worked.

- Courage, not bravery. Bravery is rooted in the physical. Courage is derived from *cor* – the Latin word for 'heart'
- Collaboration. Alpha culture can be a lonely place, but together we are stronger. We cannot be successful unless we are surrounded and supported by talented people
- Vision over ambition. The first is Michelle Obama. The second is Lady Macbeth. Take your pick
- Strength grounded in perseverance and emotional openness, not dominance and power. One builds and empowers, the other suppresses and stifles
- Excellence, not perfection. The first is a goal, the second a strait-jacket

- Balance. In everything. We are a blend of intellect, emotion and instinct. Use only one at your peril
- The bigger picture, not tunnel vision. Focusing on one goal can blind you to everything from weak spots to opportunities. Seeing the wider picture can illuminate them
- Life ambition. All of us work and have a life. Both must be in harmony to get the best out of them
- Determination – but not at any cost. We focus on goals but admit mistakes in order to learn
- Kindness can infuse everything, from how we make profit to how we treat each other at work
- Wisdom over knowledge. Combining learned facts with the lessons of experience and a deeper level of intuitive understanding makes wisdom a power that far exceeds knowledge
- Legacy, not status. One is about working to achieve long-term, sustainable goals for ourselves and others. The other is about the short-term victory of a flash title and a corner office
- Emotion, harnessed well, can be one of our greatest tools
- Caring. We give something back to those around us
- Resilience. The reed bends in turbulent winds; the oak stands stiff and breaks

They were the qualities that I, as a woman, felt reflected my best self, which was why I put them at the core of all I went on to do. And they have become the building blocks of how we restructured the culture of our business to start working like a woman.

14

Coming Together

'A wise leader does not assemble a team of only those who will agree with him, he needs someone who disagrees with him to allow him to see his blind spots.' Haemin Sumin, The Things You Can See Only When You Slow Down

Talking about values is one thing. Translating them into what you actually do every day is another. That's why I can't give you a blueprint for culture change. It's unique to every organization. But there are plenty of ideas to think about.

The tech company Satalia, for instance, has no managers or Key Performance Indicators. Even pay is transparent. The reason? Founder Daniel Hulme's core belief that the way business works should enable 'everyone to do the work they love'.

I agree that expressing what you value through how you behave changes the way you work in very tangible ways. At Portas, we didn't have to work on diversity because we naturally have a pretty even split between male and female employees. We're okay on class and sexual orientation too. The board is made up of two men, two women, and between us we're unmarried, married, middle and working class, gay and straight, parents and childless, so we're a pretty thorough mix of just about everything.

For us, though, embedding the value of collaboration into the business was a key culture change. And, given that the core of any business is money, we decided that a good place to start would be the financials – and everyone's relationship to them.

Until then, we'd been working along traditional alpha lines when it came to the numbers: the 'lower down' you were, the less you knew about money. Key financial information was kept to senior management, and while teams might have financial goals, they had no idea how these threaded into the bigger picture.

But if people had an increased understanding of the inner financial workings of the agency, we reasoned, they were bound to feel more invested in it and work together to succeed. To do that, we needed to create more financial transparency.

So, instead of splitting people into departments and telling them how much money we wanted them to make, we started to tell them about where we were as a business financially, where we believed we could get to and how we were going to do it together.

Then, rather than set financial goals at the top of the business – and implicitly tell teams to reach them come Hell or high water – we asked everyone to input. Creating collective ownership of figures makes everyone feel they have a stake in success.

Remember those Harvey Nichols board meetings that went on for hours as we pored over numbers?

Our new financial meeting was easily slotted into fifteen minutes one morning a week as we detailed quarterly and annual targets, how we had built the figures and where we were on achieving them. It wasn't shrouded in complicated graphs and PowerPoint presentations. It was delivered in simple language because, after all, it was pretty straightforward.

We now approach the numbers as collaboratively as the creative work always has been tackled and in an equally relaxed way. We don't whip people to get ideas from them. We work together to produce them. It's the same for the numbers.

We have also created a profit share so that everyone has a vested interest in the financial success of the whole agency.

As I said: this is not rocket science.

Communicating that you value collaboration can be done in many ways. Take how meetings are structured. I'd sat at many rectangular board tables during my working life where the seat you were in showed how far up the food chain you were. My agency had one of those too. I thought that was the kind of table you had to have. I tried to make mine a bit unusual by buying a hot-pink one. But it was still bloody rectangular.

Then, over supper one evening at home, I realized that everyone felt at ease sitting at the large round table in my dining room. There was no one at the 'head' of it. Why couldn't we do the same at work?

The table was hoofed from my house into the office and today you'll find some people sitting at it, others on sofas and some standing during agency meetings.

It's about showing – even in the physical environment – that you are more of a team than an army unit with different rankings.

One book that has really inspired me is called *Reinventing Organizations* by Frédéric Laloux. He's an amazing thinker who's looked at what he calls 'teal' organizations. For Laloux, these are the businesses of the future. One key way they work is by self-management — essentially a very pure form of collaboration. Many companies work this way and, in his book, Laloux looks at businesses that employ self-managing teams of everyone from nurses to car-part manufacturers and have produced spectacular results.

He believes that in this way natural hierarchies — rather than those enforced via intricate management structures — start to emerge as people take on different tasks.

When this is combined with the ability for people to be their whole selves at work and a shared sense of purpose, organizations can transform the way they work to become 'teal'.

It's fascinating stuff.

I hadn't read Laloux when we started this journey but realize now that we instinctively did much of what he talks about. And as we became more collaborative, a natural hierarchy did indeed emerge.

We're not entirely self-managing, though. A business like mine — one that's a mix of skills, roles, age and experience — still requires some form of hierarchy. It is, however, one of competency, not power, and that is a key difference. Managers are there because they can guide, train and inspire. People want to work alongside them.

Competency doesn't necessarily mean that you have to be the most senior person on the team in order to lead either. Recently, I sat in on a presentation prepared for one of our major clients by a junior staff member. He'd done a lot of research on the market the client was in during the run-up to a meeting and his passion for the subject shone through when he presented it to us internally.

We asked him if he'd like to do it for the client, who was flying in the next day, and he agreed. Up before the sparrows, he arrived at the office declaring he hadn't slept. He needn't have worried, though. The client responded wholeheartedly to his enthusiasm.

There is a health warning on collaboration: creating it can be tough at times. Collaboration can create conflict that takes energy to resolve. During the first couple of years of changing the way we worked, we spent a lot of time managing people's emotions and expectations. If being the leader of a business is like being the head of a family, I certainly sometimes thought that telling the kids to shut up and sit in the corner would be a whole lot easier than really engaging with them. Then I breathed through the aggravation and started to listen again.

We've also had to challenge our assumption that everyone would respond in the way we thought they would. In an effort to make our main creative meetings more collaborative, we introduced a weekly Creative Review. Everyone working on accounts would gather together and update on the main pieces of work moving through the business.

This was the one key meeting that I was always present at, and it gave me a chance to work with every level of the business. Instead of just working with the senior management, I was sitting down with the whole team.

So we've got the round table. We're all feeding in. Everyone has a voice. I thought we'd cracked this thing called collaboration. Then it became clear that the 'review' bit of the meeting's name made people feel as if it was an inspection or evaluation. They still felt as if they were waiting for me to sign off work – which therefore blew collaboration out of the water.

We decided to change the format to Workshop Wednesday, to communicate that this was a meeting at which we were all feeding in rather than one in which work was reviewed. It worked.

But while working more collaboratively is not without challenges, it's certainly produced far more positive effects than negative. We now draw ideas from every layer of the business in a way we didn't before. People who are employed at Portas are there because they're talented so it's vital that they have a voice. Instead of all the thinking being left to management and implemented from the top down, we now actively seed more ideas from the bottom up.

Caireen, for instance, sits down in one-on-ones with everyone in the business and asks them to put forward ideas as part of 'What would you do if you were MD for the day?' People see things from different – and interesting – perspectives.

Akio Morita, the man who made Sony among the most recognizable brands on the planet, believed in the power of collective input so strongly that he put much of the company's remarkable success down to its atmosphere of free discussion. 'A company will get nowhere if all of the thinking is left to management,' he once said.

Hear, hear, Akio.

But collaboration isn't just about generating ideas. It's also about the basics of how you employ people. Culture documents such as Netflix's are the stuff of legend these days, and ours took months of tweaking to get completely right. But we knew it was an important statement both to those already at Portas and to people who were coming into the business, which is why we worked on it so much.

Today, we've summed up the spirit of Portas and our mission as follows:

WE DO THE BEST WORK	Everything we do is driven by our desire to produce the best work we can, for our clients and for ourselves. Work that is clever, creative and commercial.
A FOCUS ON PROGRESS, NOT ACTIVITY	We're not interested in how long we spend on something or how many activities we undertake or how long we sit at our desks. What we're interested in is that we are producing the right work and are focused on the right things that make impact for our client's business and ours.
EVERYONE HAS A VOICE AND A PART TO PLAY	We're each here because we have something of worth to offer and should take time to understand and respect each other's role. We listen to each other because we all have something to contribute, no matter our position, seniority or number of days on the payroll.
WE ARE SHARERS, NOT HOARDERS	Ideas are our common currency and we share them. No campaign or piece of work is the result of one person. Everyone will have played a part. It's 'WE', not 'ME'. Together we are stronger.

USE YOUR INSTINCT	If it looks like a duck, waddles like a duck, quacks like a duck and you think it's a pig – it's probably a pig. Trust your (well-trained) intuition. Live by the belief of always balancing head-based intellect and heart-based values with gut-based instinct.
DRIVEN YET FAIR	We are ambitious. But we believe we can be the best by being ethical and respectful of each other, the people we work with and the relationships we build. Yes, that means it can sometimes get emotional and passionate but always with purpose, intellect and empathy.
WE EMPLOY RADIATORS, NOT DRAINS	Being a Portas person is special. We only want to work with passionate and clever people who give their best and get the best from those around them. It takes stamina always to be a radiator but through support of each other we believe we have a team that does this.
HONEST AND OPEN	We believe in transparency and candour, having moments of reflection and 'always on' guidance and coaching (that means giving it, receiving it and encouraging it). Demonstrating vulnerability, asking questions and admitting mistakes takes courage but it's only when we know that it is okay to fail and learn from it that we'll be brave enough to aim high.

WE DO NOT DISTINGUISH BETWEEN WORK AND PLAY	We are at our creative best when we get to bring our whole and true selves to work. From building an inspiring workplace that feeds our creativity, doing a collective downward dog at an agency yoga session, working around the school run, sharing our cultural loves with each other or volunteering at one of Mary's Living & Giving shops, we always look for ways to better integrate all aspects of our lives. Our work is our calling rather than a job.
ALWAYS LEARNING	We believe in creating a culture of learning and live by the belief that we continue to learn and grow no matter how old or experienced we are. To be experts in our sector we need to be innovators in our thinking and sponges to the world around.

To further ingrain the idea of collectivity we also did away with one-on-one annual appraisals because we felt they were rooted in judging or evaluating. Now we have career-progression plans that are based on two-way conversations looking at how people are getting on, what they're finding challenging and how the agency can work with them to fill those gaps – from paying for life coaching to courses to develop new skills.

And it's not just about what the person you directly report to thinks either. Several colleagues – from junior to senior – are asked to give their views on how someone is doing and to create a fuller picture than just a boss's impressions. After all, most of us have had a manager who we feel never gives us a break. Personalities clash. It's life. So group feedback is a safety mechanism against people feeling unfairly treated. You can hardly argue when everyone from the receptionist to the MD thinks you're a bit of an arrogant twit.

It's a way more powerful tool to see the whole of a person and their skills. And it's also a two-way street: individuals receive praise for what they're doing well and constructive criticism on what they might improve; managers get a fuller picture of their staff.

I learned years ago how important this was when I had a deputy I thought was fantastic because he was so efficient. But when the whole team sat down for a couple of drinks together after an event, tongues were loosened and I discovered that he was in fact verging on being a bully.

This guy was good at giving me what I wanted but treated everyone else badly. I soon let him go and resolved never again to sit in a separate office. Since then, I've always sat among the team, and when I want to talk to someone, I try either to go to them or sit together informally on a sofa rather than call them into an office. It's far more powerful to sit in a group of people doing great work than shut yourself away behind a closed door.

Improved collaboration had unexpected results, too – such as weeding out the odd person who was, to be frank, just not that great at their job or didn't want to pull their weight. It's easier to stay hidden behind others and their work when you're cut off from each other in a linear structure. Far harder, when everyone is feeding into work and assessments.

Strengthening collaboration has been key to creating a hierarchy that's based on competence alone at Portas. It's also about shifting work from a place that hems people in and penalizes them to one where everyone feels happy, heard and in harmony.

And I believe that is the starting point of great work.

15

Bringing Your Whole
Self to Work

*'If so many workplaces seem lifeless, it is perhaps
because we bring so little life to work.'*
Frédéric Laloux, Reinventing Organizations

I run a business based on creative ideas. These are our currency because we sell them to clients. But any kind of work can thrive on creativity because, whether you're an admin assistant or a heart surgeon, it's about thought processes and thinking innovatively. And creativity can be applied to everything from how you manage finances to how you employ and motivate staff.

Daniel Kindberg and Graeme Potter might seem an unlikely fit for my top-ten creative inspirations because one is a former army battalion commander and the other is a football manager. But they're on the list because they've put emotional intelligence at the heart of what they do – as well as creative spark.

Kindberg became chairman of the small Swedish football club Östersunds after he left the army but quit when it was relegated to the fourth tier in 2010: he was sick of the arguing and blame that followed. Then the players turned up at his house, asked him to return, and he decided to do so but start again from scratch.

When Potter became team manager, the men decided on a radical new approach in how to achieve their team's potential. For a start, they took on the players that other clubs had rejected. One had been kicked out of a big Swedish team after repeated behaviour infractions; another, who'd played in the UK, had ended up working on a building site by the age of twenty for similar reasons. Potter and Kindberg saw the talent of players who had been effectively thrown on the scrapheap and teased it back out of them.

How? Well, I guess they must be pretty good at all the physical football stuff for a start. But they also took a uniquely creative approach to training by exposing their players to culture, including art, theatre and literature. And by putting them in unfamiliar situations, they helped them to think differently and encouraged mental and emotional, as well as physical, teamwork. So far, as a team, they've done everything from writing a book and creating art to working with local refugee centres and putting on a stage show of *Swan Lake*.

How inspired was it to take all these men way out of their comfort zone, challenge them to explore different parts of their whole selves and see what happened?

It certainly worked.

Östersunds are now in the top league, won the Swedish cup in 2017 and qualified for the Europa League. The club from a tiny Swedish town even beat mighty Arsenal.

Thinking creatively, feeding the souls of their players, creating community and connection through shared experiences, produced quite extraordinary results and I, too, believe that inspired minds produce the best work.

We don't play on a football pitch at Portas but sitting inside four office walls all the time isn't necessarily the way to spark creative thought. So, just as Kindberg and Potter wanted to stretch their players, I encourage our people to get out there and see the world, connect with it in order to really understand how people are living. Only then can we give our clients the best advice on how to connect with their customers. Empathy doesn't just strengthen the bonds between a group of colleagues, it can also help you to better understand whoever your work is aimed at – or how you're doing it.

That's why we have a pot of money to fund staff travel. They apply for it by telling us what they want to go and see, why and how it will help the agency. Often they're looking at retail because that's our business, and visits to everywhere from Berlin to LA have been paid for.

We also pay for museum passes and have created a library in the office for people to browse through. Plus there is a monthly meeting called People of Portas that's all about sparking ideas and discussion rather than addressing specific projects, so pretty much anything goes.

Its core aim is for interesting people to talk about interesting stuff, so staff can go 'off topic' to talk about something that's inspired them, or we might listen to a speaker from a thought-provoking project like Art Against Knives. It's about developing people as whole beings, enabling them to expand their horizons outside what's strictly 'work'. First, because stimulated people produce better work (just ask Östersunds). Second, because I want anyone who's worked at Portas to leave the business feeling as if they've grown – not just professionally but personally too.

Once again, creating a culture that really enriches those who work in it might be a key way for smaller companies to attract the best talent away from big ones in the future. Instead of focusing on material benefits, smaller companies can work on creating a culture that feeds anything from intellect to emotion, allows different types of people to thrive, and has core values that employees can identify with in a very personal way.

And if small businesses did this, I think many would-be employees might just give up the gym membership and company car to work in a place they not only want to be but know will grow them for the future.

Authenticity is another key part of bringing your whole self to work, and no one will ever be able to do that until we stop splitting emotion from work in the way that we're currently required to.

Emotion is intrinsic to our whole self so why are we supposed to leave most of it at the office door? How can any of us ever reach our potential when we're stuffing down half of what makes us who we are? It affects us all, but particularly women as we try to fit the alpha-male type.

So, for me, a key part of working like a woman is about allowing a far greater range of emotions to be more present at work and bringing our whole selves to it. It's what experts call an inclusive culture: one in which everyone feels at home and able to stop pretending to be something they're not.

Research has shown that we all 'cover' who we are to try to fit in at work. And while you're more likely to do it if you're gay, a person of colour or a woman, almost half of straight white men do so too. Most of us, in some way, are putting on a mask when we go into work. Helping us to feel accepted as we are in the culture in which we work has been proven to produce better results.

That is why, in addition to focusing on client relationships, we have also given a lot of thought to what happens between people at Portas. And the creation of trust has allowed us to stop putting energy into being something we're not and devote it instead to tapping into our talents.

We've fostered this shared connection in different ways. There's a meeting slot called 'What Got Me Here' during which a member of staff talks about three things that got them to where they are. Who can fail to respond to the vulnerability it takes to stand up in front of colleagues and take off the mask, to talk about your family, your friendships, your failings, your dreams?

Random as it might sound, dogs have also been a great way to bring us closer because, almost without realizing it, people drop the mask in their presence. We all become a bit more human as we stop to stroke a dog and chat to its owner.

I walked into Portas the other day to find one staff member nervously waiting for a big client meeting to start. After fishing Ollie the Cavapoo out from under a desk and sticking him on her lap, she visibly relaxed within seconds.

Children do the same. So if childcare plans go south, as they sometimes do, parents can bring their kids into work. Not long ago, Mark brought his daughter with him and suddenly the guy who talks figures was a dad, a husband, a caring man.

All these things reveal different sides of people that help us to see each other as whole beings rather than work automatons.

Now, I know not all businesses can do what we've done. But it's about redefining how work can be improved in ways that suit your business. A small, but significant, thing for us is a pot of money given to junior team members to spend in whatever way they think will bring some fun to the office.

It's kind of like a flash mob for joy. Even small moments can reconnect and re-energize the whole team.

These things don't take a lot of time. But what they do is foster laughter and fun – and that in turn creates open, honest communication and emotional connection.

Work should be a place where you bring your whole self. Not just a part of it. And this kind of inclusion benefits a whole organization as well as its employees.

The psychologist John Amaechi, who works with businesses on everything from leadership to organizational culture, believes that inclusion starts with true honesty about what is happening in your business. 'Any change has to start with [. . .] a real, pragmatic, honest assessment of the status quo, and I don't think we have that,' he says. 'Inclusion is a threat. And it's a threat to a certain group of people and that group of people is not straight, white, older men. It's mediocre people. And our organizations are full of them. We call them the marzipan layer, we call them the permafrost, we know exactly who they are.

'And so it's no wonder that we don't get the kind of movement we need because we have people who are perfectly adequate at the job and don't cause enough trouble. They know how to handle appraisal and make sure that they get that [grade] four [. . .], which means that they stay where they are.'

I agree with John: our businesses are filled with people who are okay enough to stay in the job, not bad enough to justify sacking and difficult to shift.

I also agree with him that it's time to shift the marzipan layer and let real talent rise to the top by allowing people to be their whole, true selves.

*

The final layer of bringing a whole self to work is about creating a connection to the wider world, because we don't exist in isolation. For me, this involves giving something back through my business.

I'd learned at Save the Children that you get just as much out of giving as the person who receives does. Maybe more, in fact. Giving does all of us good.

I believe it also does my business good, so we try to give back in many different ways. That might be doing free work for a project we believe in, or just connecting people from the voluntary sector to businesses that will support them. We also offer free advice to small start-ups or, if we think we're not right for them, help them to access a different business that might be a better fit.

We're also working on developing a new internship scheme aimed at breaking down the class barriers in our industry through mentoring, coming into Portas to see what we do; and outreach work.

There's no doubt that middle-class kids whose parents can fund them on internships are far more likely to do them than kids with parents on a low income. It means that many industries – mine included – are becoming more and more uniform in terms of class. I'm well aware that I broke the system but many kids today will find it far harder. The internship scheme is one way to tackle this because, like it or not, certain kids have connections via their parents and others don't.

My elder son was lucky enough to have me, and I was confronted by a real dilemma about nepotism when it came to Mylo. After finishing his degree, he came to work temporarily at the agency as a junior member of the research and strategy team. He's a bright, well-qualified young man and soon Caireen and Richard said they'd like to recruit him permanently.

But I found myself with conflicting feelings about it. It was great that Mylo had done well, that the team liked him and thought him worthy of a place at Portas. But, much as I wanted to make life easy for him, I wasn't sure I'd be doing Mylo a favour. He needed to make his own way, to work somewhere that didn't have his surname over the door. I also feared there would always be a barrier to colleagues seeing him as truly one of 'them'.

I talked it over with his dad, who quite rightly said the decision was Mylo's. And in the end, of course, Mylo made the decision for me. He thanked me very much for the few months he'd spent with Portas – plus the free rent and board at home – but told me he believed it was best for him to go and do his own thing.

He left London to start a new job in Manchester and is now thriving very separately from me as he should.

Of course we all want to help out our kids. And our friends' kids. But this kind of social sponsorship is, if anything, getting more and more vital today. I'm not sure I'd have got a foot in my industry if I was trying to start out now, and while I'm never going to fix all of this, I hope the new internship scheme will encourage a different kind of talent into our business.

My contribution is small fry, though, compared to what businessman Hamdi Ulukaya is doing. Born and raised in a dairy-farming family in the Kurdish region of eastern Turkey – an area long riven by political fighting – Ulukaya never aspired to create his own company. In fact, he arrived in the US to study English in 1994 with an entrenched scepticism about American business, believing it was selfish and the gap between working people and CEOs so wide he could never be a part of the corporate world.

But when he started living in the US and saw a different side of business, Ulukaya decided he wanted to make a difference.

Fast-forward almost twenty-five years and he has done just that. Chobani yoghurt, the business he founded in 2005 that now employs 3000 people, has social conscience running through its core. From the outset, employees got full healthcare and were paid above the minimum wage. Many employees will also get shares in the business, worth more than $1 million to the longest-standing workers, when it is floated or sold.

Today 10 per cent of Chobani's profits go to charity, the company works with the local community and also small food companies with ideas to challenge what Ulukaya believes is a broken system of mass food production.

But it's his personal commitment to some of the world's most vulnerable people that really sets him apart. Some 30 per cent of Chobani workers are refugees, and Ulukaya has pledged to give the majority of his personal wealth to humanitarian causes. He's also created the Tent Foundation, which partners with businesses to give short-term assistance to, and create long-term solutions for, the global refugee crisis through hiring, training and employment initiatives worldwide. Its aim is to aid twenty million dispossessed men, women and children.

Why? Because Ulukaya believes that business can be a significant force in finding solutions that governments alone cannot come up with. 'We can move faster, think bigger, and modernize approaches to relief and resettlement that haven't changed since the 1940s,' he wrote, as business leaders prepared to gather in Davos for the World Economic Forum in 2016. 'We can do what entrepreneurs do best: hack the way we handle this problem.'

Don't underestimate the significance of what Ulukaya is doing. Refugees and the politics around them are an incendiary political topic. But here is a big corporate leader persuading others to give a very public commitment to people who are often demonized.

Ulukaya has been attacked by the far right and received death threats. There have been calls to boycott his business because of his stance. But he believes that work is a vital way to help rebuild lives torn apart by conflict. 'I can tell from my experience [that] the minute a refugee has a job, that's the minute they stop being a refugee,' he says. He's put social justice and the fair treatment of workers at the heart of what he's doing. He doesn't just talk about his values. He does something about them.

If only most businesses would do the same.

Our journey to working like a woman is definitely still a work in progress. We've been at this for four years now and probably will be for another few at least, putting in place the ideas that effect real change. Some of our ideas have been outright failures, and even when they've succeeded, it hasn't always been easy.

Take radical candour: it's more and more in vogue in business and is about being completely honest about successes and failures. There's no more smiling in meetings and then going off to bitch by the coffee machine.

We've used it and it's certainly been helpful – as long as it's underpinned with kindness. But I've also felt like cracking my head against the wall a few times when staff have been honest about the negatives and forgotten the positives. It can be frustrating.

As is the fact that even after we've done all this work to create a great working environment, people still leave. Unbelievable, right? We've had periods when a string of people have resigned around the same time, and that's tough in a small business. Some got new jobs, others were moving away, but there were certainly those who genuinely didn't want to be in our type of culture, and didn't feel comfortable at Portas.

I get it. I really do. I've certainly found all this personally challenging at times. Changing the way I'd always worked occasionally felt like digging out my emotional drains. Letting go of that core alpha belief that power and authority lay solely with me wasn't easy. Participating fully in the process and listening to my first group feedback gave me a sleepless night. Am I really that impatient? Hmm. And do I sometimes ignore the people I don't feel an obvious connection to? Yes. Sort it.

But doing all that made me realize that as much as we tell ourselves it's 'only work' we also take it very personally.

I used to feel snubbed when people resigned and told myself we were better off without them. Working like a woman has meant a whole new approach focused on maintaining connection with people even when they've gone.

I've learned to accept that great employees do leave – for life reasons, career progression, you name it – and I can't take it as a personal slight. Today I'm certainly sad to see valued people go but also proud to see them doing well in big jobs and grateful that we have provided a stepping-stone on their journey.

I, like everyone else working in the business, have learned

something from all this. I've learned to take it all less personally by being more personal, if that makes sense. And I'm glad I have because people, like businesses, wither if they remain static. We've always got to be learning to keep moving on.

Take all of what we've done to change the way we work in isolation and it might seem like throwing stones into a hurricane. But between them these changes have knitted together to create a heart to my business that it didn't have before. It's also produced brilliant results and my agency today is working better than it ever has done. We are now doing as well financially as we ever did. But, most importantly, I have a better business because it has soul. And that for me is working like a woman.

It sure beats just totting up the numbers.

16

Sharing Care

'If you always do what you always did, you will always get what you always got.' Albert Einstein

Two stories for you.

In the first, a friend called Mark is working as the head of sustainability for a big supermarket chain. He's working so much that he isn't seeing a lot of his kids and decides to do more of the school run. Arriving late at work means fighting for parking so the company has allocated some spaces to 'mums on the run'. Mark asks his boss if he can use one on the days he takes the kids to school.

'No!' his boss replies. 'They're for MOTHERS!'

In the second, Caireen is asleep in a hotel room in Sydney. She's there on a business trip when the phone rings late one night. It's someone from her son's nursery. He's sick and needs to be picked up.

'I'm in Australia,' she says. 'Have you tried my husband?'

'No.'

'Can you call him, please?'

'Of course.'

So far, so normal. Mothers are the ones who get the call first, aren't they?

Not in this case. Caireen's husband is at the top of the

contact list for their son because she travels more. But the person at the nursery is so programmed to ring mothers that what's written down in black and white doesn't compute.

More than ten years separate Mark wanting to do more of the school run and Caireen travelling to the other side of the world on business. During that time we've seen the rise of flexible and remote working, shared parenting leave and job-sharing. But apparently nothing much has changed when it comes to the expectation that women are the ones who will do the looking after.

'My partner and I are both journalists and the only way we could be more professionally equal is if we were the same person,' wrote Hadley Freeman. 'And yet I'm still seen by others as the caretaker: I'm the one the doctor calls if something is wrong and I'm the one whom other parents contact to make play dates – and by "other parents" I invariably mean "other working mothers".

'If my boys ever skip school, Ferris Bueller-style, I'll be the one the headmaster calls, even though I work in an office and my partner works from home.'

The culture of female care is still deeply ingrained in the way we live. And this has really got to change if we are ever to find a new way to work.

We've already covered childcare, haven't we? We know things are at best challenging, at worst stymieing to women and their careers. So why am I coming back to this? Because if I left you feeling a bit depressed earlier about how bleak things are right now, I'm now going to offer hope in the form of innovative ideas on how to improve them.

A key change is better options for working flexibly, and more – and cheaper – childcare. (More of that soon.) It's also critical that we examine our attitudes to who is responsible for caring for children, because while we've embraced the idea of women working outside the home, we haven't yet done the same when it comes to men working inside it.

Anne-Marie Slaughter was the first woman to become the director of policy planning for the US Department of State and wrote a book called *Unfinished Business* that's all about how we must care in the future. At the Aspen Ideas Festival in 2015, she said:

> We have liberated women and we have not liberated men [she says]. We have liberated women to be our fathers [. . .]. Our daughters are raised to be anything. [But] our sons are being raised the same way my father was.
>
> Your worth as a man is determined by what job you get, and how much money you make and how much power you wield. But [. . .] that's a half-finished revolution. [. . .]
>
> Men care just as much as women care. Men love just as much as women love. We need to get to a place where being a good man, a strong man, a sexy man, includes being a man who can say, 'You know what? I'm supporting my wife with care rather than cash.' [. . .]
>
> I've never met a male CEO who didn't have a lead parent at home. It's going to be the same for women. I think part of this has to be [that] men have to have a conversation [. . .] and have a much broader concept about what a good man is.

Couldn't have said it better myself.

Let's start by looking at flexible working because it's a really important way to help people integrate their work with caring for kids, the elderly or sick. And that's something we're going to have to do more and more of in the future if the state of social and child care right now is anything to go by.

Some 7.3 million British workers are now working flexibly – men in almost equal numbers to women – and that means anything from later start or earlier finish times to nine-day fortnights, working from home and job-shares. And it's only going to become an increasingly important feature of how we work because we know that Millennials want to work this way. If we get this right it will enable them to co-parent more than most of us do right now.

It's not a hard equation: if both of us can fit work around school and child-minding pick-ups, sick days and home-work, then we can share the job better.

Caireen works from home on Friday because she wants to have at least three full days of the week without care for her kids. I know as a mother what that means. Parents (and non-parents) at Portas are encouraged to work in a way that best suits them – whether that's flexible hours or part-time.

But there's still resistance to flexibility among many employers, particularly the large ones, who find it hard to trust employees with flexible hours because strong relationships aren't in place. The rewards, however, can be huge – particularly the staff goodwill it engenders.

So, while employers talk about being open to different ways of working, they don't seem to be seeing this through to their recruitment processes and employment practices.

While many people negotiate flexibility in jobs they're already in, just 12 per cent of positions with salaries over £20,000 are advertised as such. That doesn't show a massive commitment by employers, does it?

Make no mistake, though: this is a tough nut to crack. Some businesses just cannot offer flexible working – however much they want to. And then there's parental leave, which is another thorny issue.

More and more large businesses are now offering up to a year's paid leave, but I wonder how many women are taking it. A year out is a huge amount of time if you're ambitious to reach the top and know that someone else is often ready to jump into your spot. This length of time is also a significant stress on smaller businesses.

It's hard to know the right answer. I remember going back to work when Mylo was weeks old and it felt way too early. The night before, he lay on my chest as I sobbed because I just wasn't ready to leave him. I wouldn't want another woman to go through that.

But figuring out how to manage children and work is the same for millions of women. The world isn't filled with high flyers who get back to their desks within a week. It's filled with mothers who are trying to make life and work hang together, and businesses can do more to help them because juggling work with care isn't just about what you're paid when you're off. Just as important is how you integrate your personal and professional lives when you come back. That's why businesses have to do more than talk about this and offer financial packages.

At Portas, in addition to three months' full pay to primary caregivers of either gender who've been employed for two years or more, we also have a 'menu' of options that parents can choose from. You may need emergency childcare if yours falls through. Or a night nanny if your child is going through a bad sleeping patch. We'll provide those things.

Or you may want some career coaching, a staggered return to work or an allocated 'buddy' when you're off to help you keep in touch, as well as plan when and how you'll come back.

We want to empower people to be able to solve their own challenges rather than create a blanket policy for everyone because being a carer doesn't stop when you return to your desk. It's a lifetime job.

All the company policies in the world on flexible working and parental leave won't work if we don't get a lot more creative about childcare, and there are some fascinating ideas about possible solutions out there.

How about an insurance scheme for small and medium businesses that would cover the cost of parental leave? We all know smaller employers can be nervous about recruiting women of childbearing age, so surely this makes sense.

Or we could look at other countries, like Canada, the US and New Zealand, where 'co-produced' childcare, which sees parents offer time and help to nurseries in exchange for fee reductions of up to 50 per cent, is well established.

Most importantly, though, the government needs to sort out the exorbitant cost of childcare, and there are many ideas on how to do this.

The Women's Budget Group and the Women's Equality Party have costed out the financial implications of providing free universal childcare – and say it would pay for itself. Upfront costs would be offset by increased taxes, National Insurance and VAT payments, as well as a reduced benefits bill.

Another suggestion came from the Family and Childcare Trust and Joseph Rowntree Foundation, which detailed how parents would still pay but government subsidy would lower costs. Childcare would be free to low-income parents and fees would then scale up to a maximum of £4 per hour for those with a salary of more than £66,000.

These all sound to me like workable solutions to a crippling problem. So why isn't the government doing more about them?

Companies can also contribute, and those that take childcare seriously have proved it works every which way, from employee well-being to financially.

The outdoor-clothing brand Patagonia, well known for its environmental and social commitments, has provided onsite childcare since 1983. It says 91 per cent of the costs are recouped through tax breaks, employee retention and employee engagement. So the argument about childcare costing too much for large employers to provide doesn't seem to hold much sway, does it?

Why aren't more big corporations following in Patagonia's footsteps? I'm baffled that they're not because the effect Patagonia's childcare ethos has had on women working at the company is incredible. In the five years to 2016, every mother working there returned after having a child. The company also has around a fifty:fifty gender split in management. If that doesn't prove how critical good childcare is to women's careers then I don't know what does.

Or we could look further afield, to a small German town called Unterföhring, to see what an innovative strategy on childcare at a local level can do.

It's a suburb of Munich and home to twelve thousand residents, as well as businesses ranging from large insurance and media companies to tech start-ups and independent film production. It's also close to beautiful Bavarian countryside so there are farms, rivers, lakes and forests.

Oh. And childcare is free.

Yes. That's right. Childcare for any child aged over one and living in the town is free until they leave school, so that means full-time nursery as well as breakfast and after-school clubs.

The people of Unterföhring have this because they, as a community, decided they wanted it. (I told you it all started with one simple decision.)

German towns receive income from the businesses located there as well as from the state. But in the late 1970s, instead of choosing to build swimming pools or theatres, Unterföhring's mayor suggested fully subsidizing childcare as a way to draw more people to the town and make it prosperous.

The people of Unterföhring have remained committed to the principle of more childcare, more work, more tax, more community ever since. Today the town is packed with young families. Among them is Sonja Hein, with her husband Ralf and their three children. She is a lawyer, he is an engineer, and both work full-time.

When their children were born, Sonja took a six-month maternity leave, then split childcare with Ralf for the next six: they both worked half-days. Then all three kids went into free high-quality childcare. It's not all perfect. Sonja says that house prices have risen – which risks pricing out lower earners – and feels that many parents don't contribute a lot to a town that gives them so much. In Germany taxes are raised and distributed differently from the UK so we couldn't just cut and paste the idea.

But what impact has almost four decades of free child-care had on women in Unterföhring? Well, Sonja lives on an estate with thirty-eight houses and just one mother doesn't work. This is collective culture working at its best – a community's commitment to looking after its children well that also enables women to go to work.

Passports at the ready. Let's all move to Unterföhring.

17

Getting Dads Involved

'Nothing can ever fundamentally change for women at work until two things happen: we recognize unpaid labour for the vital work it is and fully accept that caring is a job of equals to be shared by women and men.' Me, Mary Portas

Much as I'm all about women's power, men are absolutely crucial to the childcare issue and there's no doubt that getting fathers involved benefits us all. If dads do their bit, women are off work for a shorter time so their careers and earnings are less impacted. Sharing care also alleviates the emotional burden of leaving a very young child to go back to work until you feel they're ready for formal childcare to start.

Fathers who take time off tend to be more involved long-term in their families, which has health and emotional benefits for them and their children.

We all win when it comes to getting men more involved in caring.

But while it's pretty much accepted now for them to have up to two weeks of paternity leave after a baby is born, efforts to get UK fathers to take more time off have hardly been a resounding success. Shared parenting leave (SPL) was touted as the way to do it when it was introduced in 2015 because it gives parents the right to split up to fifty weeks off work and up to thirty-seven weeks of pay.

'All right!' I hear you say. 'Let's do this!'

Don't get too excited. Only around 3 per cent of working fathers have taken it. It's not that many of them don't want to do more caring. About half of the fathers surveyed in 2017 said they would take SPL. But this time our working culture and money work against men.

A dad who takes SPL is worse off financially than a woman who goes on maternity leave. While a woman gets 90 per cent of her earnings for the first six weeks of maternity leave before statutory pay kicks in, men who take SPL are only eligible for statutory pay.

Even if dads are working for employers who offer enhanced parental leave then, as we know, they will usually be earning more – and that means taking time off has a greater knock to the family finances, which is another disincentive. Then there are all the men – mainly young or low paid – on insecure agency or zero-hours contracts who report that they have been sacked after asking about family-friendly policies.

Things are beginning to shift a little. Netflix – famous for its progressive culture – announced in 2015 that parents (NB: 'parents', not 'mothers') could take up to a year of leave on full pay after the birth or adoption of a child. Insurance giant Aviva now offers twenty-six weeks' leave on full basic pay to its employees.

Claims for sex discrimination by fathers who wanted to take SPL but discovered they would earn less than their female partners have been upheld by employment tribunals. Maybe employers will be forced to take the issue more seriously when the lawsuits start coming in.

Change is also afoot politically. In March 2018, a parliamentary committee that had been looking at the issue of working fathers lambasted 'workplace policies [that] have not kept up with the social changes in people's everyday lives'. It called on the government to look at introducing ring-fenced leave for fathers as an alternative to shared parental leave.

The pace of change is so ridiculously slow, though, that in the UK we're more than twenty years behind what some countries are doing. And guess what? It's those forward-thinking northern Europeans who have, once again, taken the lead.

More than twenty years ago, Sweden introduced a policy of non-transferable leave for fathers to encourage new dads to take a full three months at home, and it's now proposed to extend it to five. There are similarly progressive ideas coming out of Iceland and Germany, where the financial offer is much more robust.

But this is about much more than finances and legislation. Once again it's about the culture we in Britain are working in and whether a full life – which includes family as well as work – is valued.

Japan has the most generous paternity leave entitlement in the world – thirty weeks at full pay – but also a notoriously tough attitude to work. Just 2 per cent of fathers took advantage of the leave available in 2015.

The USA, the world's largest economy, doesn't have a national policy on paid parental leave yet (although, at the time of writing, Donald Trump had put forward proposals for a national policy of six weeks' paid leave for all parents). It doesn't strike me as coincidence that many fathers in these two ultra-alpha cultures either don't take the leave on offer or aren't given any at all. The commitment to overworking as a way to 'prove' worth is a major hurdle we need to get over if we want men to be more involved. Long hours are as much, if not more, of a badge of honour as they ever were in alpha culture.

The commitment to overwork is the key way in which workers 'prove' they're fit to climb the ladder, either put in voluntarily or demanded by the organization as part of an unspoken pact, and men are more likely to work those long hours than women. In many jobs more hours often equal more money – and more money means more status.

So, aside from practical measures such as improving flexible working and job-shares, the focus – yet again – must be on culture. It is vital that our dedication to the idea that more work is better work is severed. Because it's not. Even though it's been proved that regularly overworking causes a significantly increased risk of everything from strokes to diabetes, we're still tied to our desks – and phones, which means we never leave work behind. If our ancestors proved their strength by killing sabre-toothed tigers, their modern equivalent does it by refusing ever to switch off their email.

There's pressure on all of us to overwork but even more so on men: while women are 'allowed' to take time off to care, fathers who want to get more involved can be stigmatized by colleagues. MPs who talked to working dads heard that they were mocked by co-workers for going part-time to accommodate childcare pick-ups, with colleagues saying, 'Bye, part-timer', or 'Are you working part-time again?' or 'Oh, you're off early again.'

This is the message that alpha culture is sending all of us – particularly men. Changing the way we work should not be seen as tackling a 'woman's problem' – it's everyone's.

Dismantle the alpha focus on long working hours and you've taken a big step towards equality, which is why I've tackled this issue very seriously. At Portas, it's no longer a question of how long you work but how well.

We've now got systems in place to ensure that staff don't feel they should be doing sixty-hour weeks. And although we know there are busy periods in the run-up to client delivery, for instance, we wonder what's going wrong if someone is sitting at their desk night after night. It's a tough nut to crack in our industry, where long hours have been ingrained into most people. Who wants to be thought of as the 'slacker' who leaves on time every day?

But to check and balance this, we ask staff to fill in timesheets that are monitored by managers. If we see that someone is regularly working too many hours, it's flagged up and we talk to them. Either their workload is too much, they don't have the right skills to keep on top of it (which means we have to give them support and training) or a health or home issue is keeping them at their desk.

There are certainly ways to shift our culture from over-work to one that enables all of us to care more but, right now, business is not doing enough to use them.

It means that all too often, rather than share an unavoidable hit on earnings, status and promotion potential, women take it alone as it's argued that children need one primary carer rather than two equally involved ones.

And this is the chicken-and-egg conundrum that creates inequality: men earn more because they do more hours, and get promoted more because they show the 'dedication' that's needed to move upwards. Women, meanwhile, are left quite literally holding the baby – and earning less.

Removing the cultural barriers facing fathers at work is

as much about changing our own personal attitudes as it is about what happens at the office.

I'm afraid it's time for some difficult conversations across dinner tables about how much men are going to step up. And I suspect there will be quite a few who wouldn't want to care more, even if they could, because they're happy for their female partners to do it.

I understand. Looking after a baby or a small child is wonderful, rewarding and a part of life that has layers of meaning. But it's also monotonous, isolating and, at times, the most emotionally challenging work there is. I'm not surprised some men are happier to stay at work. I remember going back and almost crying with happiness when I could make a coffee without the baby monitor going off. Even getting on the Underground to go to work felt like a break.

But if we're going to reframe our attitudes to shared caring as a society, we also need to reframe them personally – and men who see equal care as a choice must start to realize that it's not. It's a responsibility.

Then we need to have an honest conversation about how they feel about getting more involved: their fears and concerns, the social pressures they face and what they can do to alleviate the desire to stab their eyes out with a fork when the *Peppa Pig* theme tune comes on for the hundredth time. Because just as women are crippled by the images of the 'perfect' mother or hampered by the notion of 'super-women' in leadership, I suspect many men are also deterred by the image of a hipster dad carrying his baby in a sling. It's not exactly a relatable image for a welder in Scunthorpe or a corporate lawyer in Edinburgh.

There are many reasons why men are less involved in childcare than women: the biology of birth and initial care, the reluctance of women to give up control, and many men's fear of being in charge of a small child. They need to be not only encouraged to take more responsibility for their children's care but supported to do so. They'll find that, by spending time with children, it's possible to acquire new skills – like empathy, patience and multi-tasking – which are of benefit in the workplace. So, too, is the inevitable new perspective about what's really important in life.

I know this is possible because Leon Barron, a lecturer in forensic science who is also one of the few fathers who's taken SPL, told me so. He's refreshingly honest: he wasn't driven by a need to be an earth dad when he took SPL. He did it because he felt responsible enough to share the care for his children with a wife who'd also worked hard at her career and he was aware that spending time with his two sons would allow them to forge a close bond. And Leon believes other men need to take a more active role in caring, too, because it benefits both their home and working lives.

Women have a part to play in getting men more involved. I know a lot of us are happy to do this caring work because we're committed to our children. But if we're serious about achieving equality at work, it's time we asked men to do more at home.

I certainly know women who think that men 'can't' care as well as they can – and that perfectionist streak really needs to be reined in. My defining moment on that came the day I left Verity with Graham while I went to work. Her school play was on that afternoon so I left work early and arrived to find kids wearing everything from princess dresses to mini suits. Then Verity appeared on stage with a mop of unbrushed hair, wearing scuffed My Little Pony trainers and worn-out lavender leggings.

'Why did you dress her like that?' I hissed at Graham, later on.

'Because she chose it,' he said innocently, and I wanted to scream that you never, ever, let a four-year-old choose their clothes on the one day when they're appearing in the school equivalent of a fashion parade.

But I didn't. I let it go. If I wanted him to do his bit, I had to let him do it in his own way, not mine.

We also need to get on top of the drive to stop inadvertently propping up the idea that this is 'our' work by making life happen as if by magic. Many of the women I know are constantly — and silently — filling the gaps. They sort out birthday parties and doctor's appointments, produce all that's needed for Christmas or the summer holiday without so much as a blink. Even twenty-something women, my daughter's age, seem to be doing the same thing by booking holidays and arranging shared social calendars.

And the moment we sigh in awe at how good a man is to take an active role in caring or look at him askance in a playground filled with mothers, we're saying, 'This is women's work.'

Instead of valiantly marching on, slowly disappearing under the weight of office deadlines, school projects, homework and organizing everyone's social diaries, women should stop asking for help as if it's a favour. Instead, we need to start seeing our relationships as a lot more equal than many of them are right now.

18

The Power of Protest

*'Unless someone like you cares a whole awful lot,
nothing is going to get better. It's not.' Dr Seuss*

If we are to change the way we work, there is one thing
I'm sure of: women must join together to create change.
We can't fix this problem on our own. I'd like us to begin
by stopping thinking of this as a 'me' problem – 'the barriers I face', 'the pay gap I can't solve', 'the positive attitude
I must maintain'. Instead, we must start seeing it more in
terms of 'we'.

Because if women started getting a little more pissed
off, or at least called out some of this stuff in the places
where we work, we could create a force for change that is
unstoppable.

As Alice Walker said: 'The most common way people
give up their power is by thinking they don't have any.'

But we do. And sometimes the most effective way of
exercising it is together.

Just imagine for a moment if every woman who is
working – for pay or not – went on strike at the same time.
Even for just a couple of hours. What would happen?

In Iceland in 1975, there was chaos when women decided
they'd had enough and took the day off to prove just how

crucial their work was. They didn't do their jobs. They didn't cook. They didn't look after their children. Men had to take their kids to work. Corner shops ran out of sausages as dads rushed to find something easy to cook for tea. And that one day put Iceland at the forefront of an equality movement that it's still leading.

'What happened that day was the first step for women's emancipation in Iceland,' said Vigdis Finnbogadóttir who, five years later, was elected president of Iceland – the first elected female head of state. 'It completely paralysed the country and opened the eyes of many men.'

Forty years later we are still having to down tools to get men to take notice of us. In 2018, more than five million women went on strike in Spain to call out inequality under the slogan 'Without us the world stops'.

Organizations and governments clearly have a key role in helping to create the conditions for change. But we, as women, also have a crucial part to play in the process. The painful truth is that we are not just the victims of all this. Sometimes we are the active architects. (Hello to all the women in HR departments who've been dealing with people's salaries for years and somehow haven't spoken up about the gender pay gap.)

Recently, I was asked by BBC Radio 4 to talk on *Woman's Hour* about the scarcity of women on retail boards, and there was a lot of chat from other women taking part about how much things were improving. They didn't sound too annoyed by what is still massive under-representation, which perplexed me. Did they really think things were sorted out? Or were they unwilling to rock the boat?

And if women who are senior and experienced enough to be asked to talk publicly on the radio about this subject don't call it out, then what hope is there for the twenty-one-year-old trainee surveyor or admin assistant?

We've all got to be prepared to start speaking up as much as we can in our day-to-day lives.

'But I can't take on centuries of patriarchy and fix it!' I hear you cry, as you shuffle off towards the TV remote. 'What can I do about all this?'

Well, nothing changes until people start saying they've had enough, does it?

Men didn't hand women the vote politely. We protested for it. Black Americans weren't suddenly welcomed into the fold of equal rights. They marched and advocated to demand them. Gay men and women drove a profound shift in public attitudes to sexuality by refusing to hide any more – just as trans men and women are doing today.

There's no magic wand. None of these issues has been completely solved. But we've got to see them in the sweep of history and recognize how much has already been done to create change. And then consider going a step further and thinking about how we can together help to drive more of it.

People can create movements, and even individual actions can spark seismic change.

Teresa Shook was incensed when a man who had bragged about grabbing women by the 'pussy' went on to be elected the most powerful politician on the planet. So, in the wake of Donald Trump's election to US president in November 2016, she posted a simple message on the Facebook page of a political group: 'I think we should march.'

This single post would morph into arguably the biggest public protest we've seen for decades: the Women's March. It lit a wildfire of support for protest that ultimately saw millions go out onto the streets in more than fifty countries to protest Trump's election and demand social change.

(It also revealed just how funny women can be when we're given a marker pen, a placard and a public platform. My highlights? 'We shall overcomb' with a picture of Trump's hairdo underneath; a placard with 'In England, Trump is another word for fart'; and the older woman who summed it all up in eleven words, 'I can't believe I still have to protest this fucking shit.')

Not so long ago we didn't have such an appetite for protest. If I'd written this book even just a few years back I suspect many of you might have wondered why I was making such a fuss. Being bored of gender inequality was about as popular as saying Crocs weren't so bad. Things had moved on, hadn't they? Women could vote and get mortgages, have sex as much as any man, were doing well at school and, between the Queen and Theresa May, we Brits had a good line going in female leadership, thanks very much.

Feminism wasn't needed any more.

But stories of women's persistent inequality and sexual harassment exploded again into public consciousness in a way they hadn't in decades when Harvey Weinstein hit the headlines in late 2017. The scandal reverberated internationally, and it became clear that it wasn't just one rogue film producer at fault but also a system that had allowed him to go unchecked for so long.

It wasn't just a Hollywood thing. As the story spread, it was as if a collective trauma was being uncovered. Stories about harassment, abuse and plain old bad behaviour did not just surface on social media, they flooded it.

And the stories of many women – and men – shared a common thread of people working in organizations and industries that had not just failed to deal with what was happening but arguably perpetuated it by sheer complacency.

When asked about Weinstein on BBC's *Newsnight*, actor Emma Thompson said: 'What I find extraordinary is this man is at the top of a very particular iceberg. He's at the top of the ladder of a system of harassment and belittling and bullying and interference. This has been part of our world, women's world, since time immemorial so what we need to start talking about is the crisis in masculinity, the crisis of extreme masculinity, which is this sort of behaviour.'

Bravo, Emma.

Suddenly women from all areas of work, from politics to the hospitality and charity sectors, started talking about their experience of people – often with power – taking advantage of those with less because of their age, status or seniority at work.

Until the Hollywood story broke, it seemed as if we had all been sleepwalking through it. We heard stories from our friends, many of us had experienced harassment ourselves, and yet it was so common, so much part of everyday life, that we were silently accepting. Then Harvey Weinstein was brought down and sexual harassment became part of the national conversation.

Following the scandal, the Equality and Human Rights Commission published the results of research they'd done. The report revealed that women were overwhelmingly the targets of sexual harassment at work and the most common perpetrators were senior colleagues. It criticized 'corrosive cultures which silence individuals and normalize harassment', as well as 'a lack of consistent, effective action on the part of too many employers'.

Interestingly, two types of women at opposite ends of the

spectrum are among the most likely to experience sexual harassment: those under twenty-eight, and women directors or board members, the weakest and the strongest in the professional power pyramid. Presumably one is an easy target and the other needs to be taken down a peg or two.

Then there is the significant problem of workplace bullying – encouraged by our all-too-often aggressive and combative workplace culture. It often stays hidden because victims are unwilling to report what is happening. Afraid that they will end up being penalized if they speak out, they have very real fears about raising concerns and coming off worse.

Of course the Weinstein story got massive attention, due to the involvement of celebrity actresses, and there was cynicism about the Time's Up campaign, soon launched by three hundred women from across the entertainment industry calling for an end to sexual assault, harassment and inequality. It was also backed by some of America's most invisible women workers. In an open letter to Time's Up, Alianza Nacional de Campesinas, which represents 700,000 female agricultural workers from across the US, wrote:

> Even though we work in very different environments, we share a common experience of being preyed upon by individuals who have the power to hire, fire, blacklist and otherwise threaten our economic, physical and emotional security.
>
> Like you, there are few positions available to us and reporting any kind of harm or injustice committed against us doesn't seem like a viable option.
>
> Complaining about anything – even sexual harassment – seems unthinkable because too much is at risk, including the ability to feed our families and preserve our reputations.

I can relate to why they daren't speak out. When I was starting at Harrods, one of my bosses invited me for supper 'to talk about how you're getting on'. It soon became clear there was only one thing he wanted me to get on when he exposed himself in his car. I made my excuses and ran for a tube. But after telling some of the girls at work about what had happened, I found out he'd done the same to them.

I didn't confront him about his behaviour or report it. I needed my wage to survive so I had to ignore what he'd done. Just as, at other times, I had to brush off the inappropriate jokes or being sworn at in a way male colleagues never were.

Critics of Time's Up questioned whether actresses walking the red carpet with activists was the 'right' kind of feminism. Certainly for me the most radical protest was seeing Frances McDormand stepping up onto the Oscar podium to accept her best actress award amid a sea of women who looked as if they'd been sleeping in a cryotherapy chamber for weeks. She wore almost nonexistent make-up, her hair looked as if she'd cut it herself, and she was fabulous.

Cannibalizing ourselves about the right way to protest is missing the point: sexual harassment is an issue that affects many women at work, and just by talking about it we're sending a message that it's unacceptable. The Weinstein story revealed fatal flaws in alpha culture: namely, a power structure that leaves those at the bottom of it voiceless and a lack of action by leaders to solve the problem.

The mandatory reporting of the UK's gender pay gap in 2018 revealed similar themes. There was huge debate; critics called the whole thing a meaningless exercise in arbitrary data collection. But it was undoubtedly a watershed moment in the discussion about women and work.

There it was in black and white. Just how much less women earn on average in relation to men because of all the reasons we've covered – taking breaks to care for children, doing more low-paid work, and just common-or-garden discrimination. Barely one in ten UK women earn equal to or more on average than their male colleagues.

Keep that stat in your head. Barely one in ten of us.

Amid all the soul-searching, a piece by the BBC journalist Sarah Montague in the *Sunday Times* stood out for me. She described how she'd worked as a presenter on the *Today* programme for almost twenty years before discovering she was being paid less than her male colleagues when the BBC was forced to disclose the names of its highest-earning stars. 'I felt a sap,' she wrote. 'For years I had been subsidizing other people's lifestyles.'

I'd say a lot of women are feeling like this: from cleaners and care workers to lawyers and CEOs. And it's not just about the money they earn. It's about feeling their trust has been systematically abused.

I have no idea how the events of 2018 will play out. Will the momentum be sustained? Or will it tail off as we turn our attention to the next big thing?

I hope not.

I'd like to see this conversation carry on in any way it can: in newspapers and magazines, on television and radio, through formal and informal channels at work, in Parliament and business organizations, between all of us on social media.

And while #metoo and #timesup focus on sexual harassment, and #genderpaygap tackles what we earn, maybe it's time for #WorkLikeAWoman to talk about equality at work.

We can use it to come together to talk about everything from bullying to unequal pay, being passed over for promotion, doing jobs that are not economically valued, and not getting enough say at the top of organizations about how to drive change.

And elsewhere, within our own workplaces and personal lives too, we can make changes, however small. Have some tough conversations with your partner about who is going to care for children, if you haven't yet had them, or how things might change, if you already have.

Talk to other women in your office about what is happening with them, the inequalities they see, and come up with some small but significant suggestions about how your workplace might better operate. Then take them to your manager together.

Don't book the meeting room, sort out the coffee or take the notes. It's not 'your' work. Support other women in meetings to get their points across, and back them up if they are being sidelined.

Change is not happening fast enough. We've got to get more vocal and play a part in creating it. It's more than possible to radically shift attitudes to what previously seemed 'normal'.

Not so long ago, we were chucking anything and everything in the bin, drinking takeaway coffees in plastic-lined cups, and wouldn't be seen dead with a hessian shopping bag in place of a plastic bag. Now, after seeing the devastation wreaked on marine life by single-use plastics in *Blue Planet 2*, many of us have vowed to never use them again.

The issue got to the top of the political and business

agenda because people had had enough. In response, UK supermarkets have pledged to ban all but essential single-use plastics by 2025.

We have profoundly shifted the way we think about the environment. Surely now it's time to do the same for driving change in the way we work.

Joining forces with other people (men as well as women because I've hopefully convinced you that all this will benefit them as much as us) collectively to create change will be the most powerful starting point. And you can do this anywhere from a shop floor to a boardroom.

You don't have to be wealthy or famous – just supremely pissed off.

Here's your new motto: JFDI. Just fucking do it.

19

#WorkLikeAWoman: The Guide

'I'm not gonna spend the rest of my life working my ass off and getting nowhere just because I followed rules that I had nothing to do with setting up, okay?' Tess McGill, Working Girl

We've looked at what government and business can do to start making work more equal. We've examined how the men in our lives have a critical role to play in all this and how we, as women, can come together to support each other.

And now it's about you, because that's where all of this truly starts.

Be warned: to reach your fullest potential will require hard work and determination. I spent years funnelling a lot of that in the wrong direction as I tried to fit in. So, the most valuable piece of advice I can give you is this: be wholly, unapologetically, wonderfully you – not who you think you need to be.

You're going to need courage to dare to stand up to the system but you will find it – in even the smallest of ways – at whatever stage of your working life you're at.

So here it is, the advice my present self would have given my younger self at different stages of my career. Plus some tips for women who are my age and older. They all come with one important health warning: I've grouped them into the loose career stages you might be at during different decades of your life. But if you're not a mother by the time you hit your thirties or a leader in your forties, don't panic. We all develop at different speeds.

For Twenty-Somethings

Keep your sense of humour. Work is serious but you're going to have to laugh off a whole lot of ridiculous stuff

Don't ask your mum to ring up and ask for a place on an internship scheme. Do it yourself. You're a grown-up. And behave like one, if you're still living at home, by paying your way and doing your own washing

You have choices. Think carefully about the kind of place where you want to work. Ask questions of your employer. Research the company you might work for. What are their staff retention rates? (Happy people don't leave jobs in droves.) What's their parental-leave policy? How many women do they have in senior management?

The working world might make you feel like a tiny cog but if you are good at what you do you are an asset. Businesses need you every bit as much as you need them. Never feel inferior

But never act entitled. No one is doing you a favour by employing you and you're not owed anything either

Whatever you do, whether it's waiting tables or becoming a trainee barrister, take pride in it and do it to the best of your ability. Challenge yourself

Make small, vital decisions every day about how you work and interact with people. Be polite, be kind and keep the moaning to a minimum. It drains your energy – and that of those around you

Work is a question of hard graft, talent and luck. The first you can control. The second two you can't. Make the most of whichever pieces of this puzzle you get

Support other women: your colleagues are your greatest strength, not your enemies

Whether you have a job or a career, this is a long road. Be patient

Education isn't everything. The decisions you make in your twenties can have the biggest effect on the rest of your life — both professionally and personally. Be thoughtful

Don't worry if you don't know where you're going. You will. And if you don't have a sense of direction by about twenty-eight, it's probably time to find one

Establishing relationships is key. Turning up to the opening of an envelope to 'network' or going to the pub with colleagues week in week out to keep on top of gossip isn't. Also resist the temptation to make too many 'baggage friends' who are just there for the good times

We don't all have careers. Some of us have jobs that support the rest of our life. And that's fine

Don't move in with a man who thinks equality means splitting the bill for dinner and leaving you to do all the running of a home

Have faith in what you do. A responsible attitude, the willingness to take a risk, curiosity and dependability will always shine through

Don't overspend on your credit card. Debt ties us down — and keeps us in jobs we don't want to do just to pay off the bills

You don't need an app or a life coach to give you the confidence to speak. It is there within you. The world today can suck a lot of power from you. Find yours

Keep organized. You can waste a whole lot of precious work — and life — time if you're not

Be courteous but courageous. Speak up, speak out, be bold in your ideas

For Thirty-Somethings

Be self-aware. Very self-aware. Take time to understand your true values and try your very best to follow them

Don't confuse overworking with promotion potential. Progress, not activity, is what counts. Few bosses will penalize someone who produces but isn't tied to their desk

Motherhood does not give you a pass to be afraid. I once offered a job to a pregnant woman and discussed how we'd work with her to combine a new job with motherhood. But she decided to stay in a job she wasn't happy in rather than take a risk

Be original. If you're moving up the ladder, your boss has seen something in you. Don't become a one-size-fits-all executive because you think that's the way you 'must' be. There are far too many of them out there already

Don't be afraid of your ambition. You're entitled to it

When I offer women a promotion, they often wonder if they're up to the job. Men ask what the pay rise is. Go figure

If you have had children and can afford to stop working, think carefully about becoming a stay-at-home mum. Earning your own living gives you independence

If you work and have children, build a network of support via friends, neighbours and other parents. No one can be an island

If you're the mother of small children, on the days your eyeballs feel about to bleed remember that this, too, shall pass

If you're childless, don't think work is where all your focus should be. Make sure your life outside work is rich: it will make you so much more interesting to employ and happier personally

The emperor often really does have no clothes. Those who get promoted aren't always the best talent. They're just good at putting a wrapping on it. Claim your successes

Choose your partner well. If you aspire to reach the top, you will need support, practical help and kindness from whomever you share your life with

Always trust your intuition – whatever anyone else is telling you

It's understandable to feel you have to fit in at the beginning of your career. Now's the time to start realizing that you don't always have to

Create your own micro-culture. Even if you're in charge of just one person, you have the chance to manage them in a way that reflects your values

Don't feel grateful for making work work for you. Whether it's flexible hours or working part-time, no one is doing you a favour. You don't need to keep thanking them

Always be a team player but never be the one who always says yes. There is a line between helpful and passive

For Forty-Somethings

By now you may be becoming more senior with more responsibilities, and everyone gets imposter syndrome now and again. The key is to recognize whether you have genuine doubts or if you're self-sabotaging

If you've had children and gone part-time, remember that you're not being paid for a full-time job. Work your hours – and resist the temptation to 'keep up' with people who are in the office more than you

We are all afraid of failure. But men don't let it hold them back as much. We need to learn this lesson too

Break some rules. If you haven't got 100 per cent of the qualifications needed for the promotion then still apply

Don't get mentors, get sponsors. Talking is easy but you will need people who actually champion you. Whoever they are, they are vital to moving upwards. Most people feel flattered to be asked to get involved

Put on your own oxygen mask first. Being senior or a leader takes a lot of energy. Look after yourself by taking time to relax, exercise and sleep

Take your responsibility to the women lower down the pipeline seriously. What you do and what you enable others to do will send vital messages to all those in your organization

You will always be learning – however high you climb. If you need help, ask for it from those you trust

Recruit people. Not CVs. Get creative about hiring. If you believe in diversity, enact it

You may now be in a position to look at the way your organization works and challenge it. Ideas translated into action can shift the status quo

Separation, divorce and parenting teenagers could all be realities for you by now. If you thought you'd be a CEO but have fallen short, you are not failing. You are living a real life

Value difference. Not just in gender, race or class but in personality too. It takes all kinds of attributes to make a team

Choose the people you work with carefully – be they clients or colleagues. If they share your values then life will be a whole lot easier

Believe in what you are doing. Communicating confidence in anything from an unusual business strategy to a new way of working will inspire it in others – clients as well as employees

Be honest about who you are. This will give those you lead the most powerful permission there is to be themselves, too

Emotions are not the enemy. In a world of robotic senior leaders, use your passion and energy to inspire others

Keep working on that sense of humour. You'll need it now more than ever

For Fifty+-Somethings

To infinity and beyond, as Buzz Lightyear would say. The reason there's no age limit in this category is that I genuinely do not see my working life as a door that will close at 'retirement' age. I see it as a part of my life which will continue for as long as I want it to

That said, if you've earned enough to be financially secure, make sure not to cling too hard to the big salary and forget the rest of life. It's finite. Enjoy it

You might by now be a senior leader so forge relationships with other women who are too – within your organization or without. Rising up can be lonely

You are never too senior to admit when you're wrong. Say sorry. Admit that you messed up, fix it and move on

Keep an open and curious mind. No one wants someone sitting in the corner of the office saying they've seen – and know – it all

On the other hand, though, know that there is wisdom in experience and use it gently

Keep positive. The world at large might make you feel invisible but you're not

Learn from your younger colleagues. Listen carefully to their life view, their aspirations and priorities – they will challenge and inspire you

Keep yourself fit and active. It's crucial to me to keep my energy levels up so I walk, do Pilates and yoga

Give really focused time to the bits of your work that make your soul sing. You've been working for a few decades now so it's time to do what makes you happy

You need to open up to let the new in so de-clutter – whether that's friends or ideas you've held on to for a long time but are now weighing you down

Let go of some responsibility. You don't have to do it all

Don't be ruled by a structured timetable. At this age, life can get really full but don't be hemmed in by excessive routine

Don't be fooled that no one can do what you do. Trust others: delegate

If you haven't reached the top and are dying to retire, remember that work isn't always paid. Unpaid work can be vital, rewarding and stimulating. You may retire from a job but you don't need to leave work

Don't forget that it's never too late to start a whole new exciting chapter of your working life

And there it is, a working life by Mary Portas. Live by it, edit it or chuck it. It's yours to do with as you want.

Now go fly.

AFTERWORD

'We have before us the glorious opportunity to inject a new dimension of love into the veins of our civilization.' Martin Luther King Jr

My younger son, Horatio, has grown up in a home with two mothers so I thought he'd be way ahead when it came to seeing women as powerful, equal figures to the men in his life.

Then he started school and my illusions were shattered.

No matter what he'd learned at home, he was now socializing in a world that was telling him in a thousand tiny ways that the female of the species is lesser. Suddenly pink was a 'girly' colour. Muscles and strength were the key indicators of his maleness. Boys were 'better'.

I'm not too worried about him. You don't live with two working mothers and end up an adult man who thinks women aren't capable and talented.

But for me, the ideas that Horatio is encountering out in the world are at the heart of the challenge facing us if we truly aspire to working like the women we are. To do so, we must shift our perception of the female away from distortions that have been centuries in the making and still hold much sway. We must value feminine power every bit as much as masculine, instead of sidelining or crushing it.

Right now, though, girls are still learning from a very young age that they are inferior. Why else would those as young as six be less likely to think women are intellectually brilliant? Or be more reluctant to take part in games for 'clever' kids?

We are weighing down our daughters with a legacy of inferiority, crippling fear of failure and unwillingness to take risks in order to avoid making mistakes. Girls who are so anxious to achieve academically that they feel a heavy weight of responsibility from a very young age.

They are also living in a world that is telling them, perhaps more powerfully than ever before because of the proliferation of technology, that their primary power is their physical appearance – not intellectual or emotional strength. Then they end up in a working culture they have to fight against: whether they want to reach the top or simply do a job that is currently undervalued because it's 'women's work'. Many will also, one day, combine this with doing the majority of care for their children. No wonder they are stressed and anxious.

Meanwhile the young men in our lives are suffering too: performing less well in education than girls, less likely to crack their tough façade by admitting a mental-health problem, more likely to commit suicide. Many also sacrifice family life in favour of work and crush the caring and intuitive aspects of their nature.

To raise young men up, we must teach them that achieving personally by being fully engaged in their families is every bit as worthy as professional success. We must give them a more complex understanding of masculinity than tough super-heroes, while ensuring they do not feel demonized for their masculinity.

To raise young women up, we must teach them that they are as strong, capable and courageous as our sons; we must allow them to be as competitive and ambitious as boys; we must show them that they are allowed to mess up, and dress down, as much as boys are.

This is what will create more equality between young men and women. And allow women to claim not just their rightful share of our working world in the future, but also of the very creation of the future itself.

Power will lie in technology in years to come but women are not yet equally responsible for creating it. If we want the future to be more equal, we must make technology that is equal – not created in the likes of the men currently developing it.

Economics intimately affects our daily lives, too, but here as well women are under-represented. Just one in four students applying to study the subject at university is female and men still largely formulate economic policy.

To solve all this, we must think carefully about the messages we are sending our daughters and encourage them not to shy away from 'hard' topics, like economics or science, at school, to want to go into these industries and take guardianship of decisions in the interests of other women.

We must raise them to apply for mortgages as adults, pay for dinner on a date, ask for a pay rise, and not leave the men in their lives to manage household finances while they unload the washing-machine. Then women will step up and take responsibility in the public world of money in the same way that we're asking men to do in the private world of care.

Because when men and women become equal partners in life as well as work, we will create a different kind of world: one in which the masculine and the feminine are merged to become even stronger together than they are apart.

And I genuinely feel hopeful that this is going to happen.

We cannot continue as we are. Our systems, values and behaviours are at breaking point, and ordinary men and women are expressing their dissatisfaction with the status quo more and more frequently.

Working like a woman is not about replacing an alpha system with an exclusively feminine one. It's about learning to value the power of feminine characteristics, embracing them in the way we work and blending the best of both genders to make us all more productive, powerful and in harmony.

It will create a kinder, more freeing and collaborative future for us all. It is not simply the way for women to reclaim their power. It's a way for all of us to do so.

Men and women have as much to gain as each other from creating radical change in the way we work and live.

This is not us or them. This is we.

NOTES

viii Just one of the nine members of its current committee is a woman. A mere six of our 100 biggest companies are headed by a woman: https://www.theguardian.com/commentisfree/2018/may/23/britain-productivity-crisis-meghan-duchess-female-empowerment

4 we've only got 10 per cent of the positions on retail executive boards: https://www.elixirr.com/wp-content/uploads/2016/06/The-commercial-advantage-of-more-women-in-the-boardroom.pdf

5 we've already outperformed boys at school and are 35 per cent more likely than them to go to university: http://www.hepi.ac.uk/wp-content/uploads/2016/05/Boys-to-Men.pdf

6 We earn less: 81p for every £1 that a man makes: https://d3n8a8pro7vhmx.cloudfront.net/womensequality/pages/2512/attachments/original/1495027355/WE_3495_Manifesto_2017_V5_Singles.pdf?1495027355

6 making up nearly three-quarters of the entry workforce and holding just 32 per cent of director-level posts: https://www.managers.org.uk/about-us/media-centre/cmi-press-releases/men-forty-percent-more-likely-than-women-to-be-promoted-in-management-roles

7 Meanwhile men are far more likely to do twenty-six of the thirty highest-paying jobs, including chief executive,

architect and computer engineer: https://www.nytimes.
com/2016/03/20/upshot/as-women-take-over-a-male-
dominated-field-the-pay-drops.html

7 **When they became biologists, the wages dropped by 18 per cent:** Ibid.

8 **Men moved into the industry and programming suddenly got way more complex:** Nathan L. Ensmenger, *The Computer Boys Take Over: Computers, Programmers, and the Politics of Technical Expertise* (Cambridge, Mass, MIT Press, 2010).

8 **The nerd was born, recruitment started to favour men:** https://www.theatlantic.com/magazine/archive/2017/04/why-is-silicon-valley-so-awful-to-women/517788/

8 **The nerd was born, recruitment started to favour men and pay increased:** Ruth Oldenziel, *Making Technology Masculine: Men, Women, and Modern Machines in America, 1870–1945* (Amsterdam, Amsterdam University Press, 1999).

8 **Today women hold just one in four jobs in the industry:** http://www.aauw.org/resource/get-the-solving-the-equation-report

8 **The education workforce is two-thirds female but in the UK male teachers earn on average £2 more per hour than women:** https://assets.publishing.service.gov.uk/government/uploads/system/uploads/attachment_data/file/477360/UKCES_Gender_Effects.pdf

8 **Women didn't enter formal employment *en masse* until about fifty years ago, and today we're almost half of the workforce:** https://data.worldbank.org/indicator/SL.TLF.TOTL.FE.ZS

8   **More than 70 per cent of UK women aged sixteen to sixty-four work:** https://www.ons.gov.uk/employmentand-labourmarket/peopleinwork/employmentandemployeetypes/timeseries/lf25/lms

8   **It's a trend seen everywhere from Japan and Germany to the US:** https://stats.oecd.org/Index.aspx?DataSetCode=LFS_SEXAGE_I_R

9   **But even though the fashion industry was worth almost ten times what the Premier League was to the UK economy in 2014:** The Premier League was worth £3.4 billion in 2014, as reported in http://www.ey.com/Publication/vwLUAssets/EY_-_The_economic_impact_of_the_Premier_League/$FILE/EY-The-economic-impact-of-the-Premier-League.pdf. The fashion industry contributed £28 billion to the UK economy in 2014, as stated in http://www.britishfashioncouncil.com/pressreleases/London-Fashion-Week-September-2017-Facts-and-Figures.

11 **two paramedics were needed on standby at the Chicago Board of Trade in case physical fights broke out:** Caitlin Zaloom, *Out of the Pits: Traders and Technology from Chicago to London* (Chicago, University of Chicago Press, 2010).

11 **and perhaps that's reflected in the fact that women still make up only 15 per cent of the financial trading workforce:** http://www.cityam.com/240774/quality-not-quantity-heres-why-women-make-better-traders

12 **They also saw an alpha-male management culture that rewarded those who were loud or aggressive in pursuing their career, leaving others behind:** https://www.secretintelligenceservice.org/wp-content/uploads/2015/07/Women-in-the-UK-Intelligence-Community.pdf

12　from just the right quarry in Kansas, and has been carefully distressed, like a pair of jeans: http://www.slate.com/blogs/xx_factor/2017/05/16/apple_s_new_headquarters_apple_park_has_no_child_care_center_despite_costing.html

13　But we're half the workforce and only a third of its managers, directors and senior officials: https://www.ons.gov.uk/employmentandlabourmarket/peopleinwork/employmentandemployeetypes/articles/womeninthelabourmarket/2013-09-25

13　If women have to acquire all the characteristics of a corporate world, it's probably not worth it: https://greatergood.berkeley.edu/article/item/are_women_more_ethical_than_men

15　The accident rate fell by 84 per cent. Productivity, efficiency and reliability improved: https://hbr.org/2008/07/unmasking-manly-men

15　and started doing 'blind' auditions by asking musicians to play behind a screen to hide their identity: Claudia Goldin and Cecilia Rouse, 'Orchestrating Impartiality: The Impact of "Blind" Auditions on Female Musicians', *American Economic Review*, 90:4 (2000).

15　Today more than half of the players in the top 250 US orchestras are women: https://www.vnews.com/Why-more-women-are-winning-at-musical-chairs-3692000

19　When two professors at Columbia Business School and New York University gave their students the same case study: Kathleen L. McGinn and Nicole Tempest, 'Heidi Roizen', *Harvard Business School* Case 800-228, January 2000 (Revised April 2010), https://www.hbs.edu/faculty/Pages/item.aspx?num=26880

19 **Half the students were told the venture capitalist was called Howard and half that she was called Heidi:** Sheryl Sandberg, *Lean In: Women, Work, and the Will to Lead* (London, WH Allen, 2015).

20 **'He is eight and a half times better than me at writing the same book':** https://jezebel.com/homme-de-plume-what-i-learned-sending-my-novel-out-und-1720637627

20 **If they do, they're less likely to approve it:** https://www.weforum.org/agenda/2016/02/women-are-seen-as-better-coders-than-men-but-only-if-they-hide-their-gender?utm_content=buffer87c0a&utm_medium=social&utm_source=plus.google.com&utm_campaign= buffer

20 **The search engine also displays six times fewer adverts for high-paying executive jobs if it thinks you're a woman:** https://www.washingtonpost.com/news/the-intersect/wp/2015/07/06/googles-algorithm-shows-prestigious-job-ads-to-men-but-not-to-women-heres-why-that-should-worry-you/?utm_term=.7e039bcaaa06

20 **'masculine values and the life situations of men who have dominated in the public domain of work':** https://www.hbs.edu/faculty/Publication%20Files/09-064.pdf, p. 2.

30 **Just 4 per cent of all MPs are women of colour, for instance:** http://researchbriefings.parliament.uk/ResearchBriefing/Summary/SN01156

30 **The problem goes even deeper, though, with far fewer women sitting on powerful select committees:** http://www.bristol.ac.uk/media-library/sites/news/2016/july/20%20Jul%20Prof%20Sarah%20 Childs%20The%20Good%20Parliament%20report.pdf

30 Some 45 per cent of female MPs are childless compared to 28 per cent of male: http://www.bristol.ac.uk/media-library/sites/news/2016/july/20%20Jul%20Prof%20Sarah%20Childs%20The%20Good%20Parliament%20report.pdf

31 We now hold 29 per cent of positions on the boards of FTSE 100 companies – compared to just 12 per cent in 2011: https://www.gov.uk/government/news/record-number-of-women-on-ftse-100-boards

31 in 2016 women of colour held a paltry thirty-seven of a total 1050 directorships in FTSE 100 companies: http://www.ey.com/Publication/vwLUAssets/A_Report_into_the_Ethnic_Diversity_of_UK_Boards/$FILE/Beyond%20One%20by%202021%20PDF%20Report.pdf

31 'We've already got one of those' and 'All the good ones have gone': https://www.gov.uk/government/news/revealed-the-worst-explanations-for-not-appointing-women-to-ftse-company-boards

37 More than a third felt it was impossible to 'be nice' and reach the top, while a fifth felt that women had to act ruthlessly to be respected at work: https://www.telegraph.co.uk/women/womens-business/10306864/Women-feel-need-to-act-like-men-to-get-ahead-at-work.html

38 One in four women says the senior women in her organization conform to a dominant and controlling 'alpha' type: Ibid.

45 I think they are more emotionally intelligent and, if you like, I think there is more intuition in the room: https://www.secretintelligenceservice.org/wp-content/uploads/2015/07/Women-in-the-UK-Intelligence-Community.pdf, p.11.

45 it's the way the human body is linked to a bigger experience and context: https://www.dwell.com/article/trend-forecaster-li-edelkoort-shares-her-thoughts-on-the-radically-evolving-design-industry-20833b31

46 Project 28-40, the UK's largest ever survey of women in work, found that 70 per cent have the desire to lead: https://gender.bitc.org.uk/system/files/research/project_28-40_the_report.pdf

46 KPMG found that we also share the same ambitions as men in many key areas: https://home.kpmg.com/content/dam/kpmg/pdf/2015/04/Cracking-the-code.pdf

46 KPMG discovered that men and women share all these key professional ambitions: Ibid.

47 'Women are more demanding and wide-ranging in their definition of success than men': https://home.kpmg.com/content/dam/kpmg/pdf/2015/04/Cracking-the-code.pdf, p. 6.

47 Roberts said he didn't spend 'any time' on gender issues in his agencies: https://www.businessinsider.de/kevin-roberts-on-women-in-leadership-roles-2016-7?r=UK&IR=T

47 They hold just 12 per cent of these roles in the UK: https://www.campaignlive.co.uk/article/creativitys-female-future/1428824

47 and 29 per cent in the US: http://www.3percentmovement.com/wherewestand/

48 'I don't want to manage a piece of business and people, I want to keep doing the work': https://www.businessinsider.de/kevin-roberts-on-women-in-leadership-roles-2016-7?r=UK&IR=T

54 **we spend double the amount of time on housework and childcare as men do:** https://visual.ons.gov.uk/the-value-of-your-unpaid-work/ and http://www.pewresearch.org/fact-tank/2017/06/15/fathers-day-facts/

54 **you're still 3.5 times more likely to do all or most of the household work than male breadwinners:** https://womenintheworkplace.com

54 **In fact, the unpaid work we do in the home is valued at around £77 billion a year:** https://d3n8a8pro7vhmx.cloudfront.net/womensequality/pages/2512/attachments/original/1495027355/WE_3495_Manifesto_2017_V5_Singles.pdf?1495027355

55 **fathers have at least tripled the time they spend with their kids over the past fifty years:** http://www.pewresearch.org/fact-tank/2018/06/13/fathers-day-facts/ and https://publications.parliament.uk/pa/cm201719/cmselect/cmwomeq/358/35804.htm#_idTextAnchor003

55 **'And if you lose that, you don't become a loser, it's just the status quo':** https://www.independent.co.uk/life-style/health-and-families/breadwinner-study-men-women-health-well-being-christin-munsch-sociology-connecticut-a7199911.html

56 **74 per cent of same-sex couples shared the responsibility compared to just 38 per cent of heterosexual couples:** http://www.familiesandwork.org/downloads/modern-families.pdf

56 **more a division of tasks according to who wants to do what:** Perlesz, Amaryll et al., 'Organising Work and Home in Same-sex Parented Families: Findings from the Work Love Play Study', *Australian and New Zealand Journal of Family Therapy* 31:4 (2010).

58 **English mothers with kids at home have seen the largest increase in employment rates over the past twenty years:** https://www.ons.gov.uk/employmentand labourmarket/peopleinwork/employmentandemployeetypes/ articles/familiesandthelabourmarketengland/2017

58 **Nearly three-quarters of mothers now work and there are fewer and fewer stay-at-home mums:** Ibid.

58 **until our children are eleven or older, we're more likely to work part-time than full-time:** Ibid.

58 **and the hourly rate for part-time work tends to be lower than that for full-time:** https://www.ons.gov.uk/ employmentandlabourmarket/peopleinwork/earningsand workinghours/articles/howdothejobsmenandwomendoaffect thegenderpaygap/2017-10-06

58 **Part-timers don't see the same kind of year-on-year salary increases that full-timers do either:** https:// www.ifs.org.uk/publications/10364

59 **The UK's average gender pay gap for full- and part-time workers is 18 per cent:** https://www.ons.gov.uk/employ mentandlabourmarket/peopleinwork/earningsandworking hours/articles/howdothejobsmenandwomendoaffectthe genderpaygap/2017-10-06

59 **women were earning on average about half what men earned:** http://uk.businessinsider.com/barclays-gender-pay-gap-bonus-2018-2

59 **Because most pilots are men and they earn the biggest salaries:** http://corporate.easyjet.com/~/media/Files/E/ Easyjet/attachments/easyjet-gender-pay-gap-report-november-2017

59 **while men do more of the more lucrative head-office jobs:** https://www.drapersonline.com/news/phase-eight-defends-gender-pay-gap/7028456.article

59 **the World Economic Forum predicts the economic gap between men and women won't close in Western Europe until 2078:** 'At the current rate of progress, the overall global gender gap can be closed in 61 years in Western Europe', http://www3.weforum.org/docs/WEF_GGGR_2017.pdf, p. viii.

61 **54,000 pregnant women lose their jobs each year because of unfair and unlawful treatment:** https://www.equality humanrights.com/en/managing-pregnancy-and-maternity-workplace/pregnancy-and-maternity-discrimination-research-findings

61 **criticisms of our statutory maternity pay as among the lowest in Europe:** https://www.tuc.org.uk/news/uk-relegation-zone-decently-paid-maternity-leave-europe-warns-tuc

61 **three in five mothers are at risk of this – and will earn up to a third less:** https://www.pwc.co.uk/economic-services/women-returners/pwc-research-women-returners-nov-2016.pdf

62 **Younger women now out-earn younger men:** https://www.ons.gov.uk/employmentandlabourmarket/peoplein work/earningsandworkinghours/articles/understandingthe genderpaygapintheuk/2018-01-17

62 **the gender pay gap starts to open after we hit forty:** https://www.bbc.co.uk/news/business-42723960

62 **It's widest by the time we're in our fifties:** https://www.ons.gov.uk/employmentandlabourmarket/peopleinwork/

earningsandworkinghours/articles/understandingthegender
paygapintheuk/2018-01-17

62 **the average woman will be earning almost a third less than the average man twenty years after having her first child:** 'Twenty years after the birth of their first child, a woman's hourly wage will on average be a third lower than the hourly wage of a man', https://www.ifs.org.uk/publications/10364

62 **but also might be because they're seen as more committed and responsible:** http://content.thirdway.org/publications/853/NEXT_-_Fatherhood_Motherhood.pdf

63 **British parents spend a mind-boggling eight times more of their income on childcare than Swedish parents:** Swedish parents spend just 4.4 per cent of their income on childcare compared to 33.8 per cent in the UK, https://www.weforum.org/agenda/2016/12/childcare-cost-oecd/

63 **Childcare costs have risen four times faster than average pay since 2008:** https://www.tuc.org.uk/news/cost-childcare-has-risen-four-times-faster-wages-2008-says-tuc

63 **And there aren't enough nursery places:** https://www.familyandchildcaretrust.org/childcare-survey-2017

63 **Those working outside a normal nine-to-five pattern, like nurses or shop workers, face even bigger problems finding a place:** https://www.familyandchildcaretrust.org/childcare-london-parents-atypical-work-patterns-what-are-problems-and-how-should-we-fix-them

63 **less than a fifth of areas have sufficient spaces for disabled children:** just 18 per cent of areas have sufficient spaces for disabled children https://www.familyandchildcaretrust.org/childcare-survey-2017

63 **including thirty hours of free childcare per week for working parents, who earn less than £100,000 per year, of three- to four-year-olds:** Tax-free childcare sees the UK government topping up money that parents pay into a dedicated account for childcare costs while thirty hours' free childcare is available for three- to four-year-olds whose parents are working and as long as neither of them has a taxable income over £100,000

63 **Low-income parents are still struggling to pay – even with the free care they get:** Low-income parents faced an average shortfall of £60 a week after claiming all the help with costs they were entitled to, https://www.family andchildcaretrust.org/childcare-prices-surge-double-rate-inflation-undermining-government%E2%80%99s-new-investments.

63 **because the money the government pays them for the 'free' care doesn't cover what it costs to provide:** The Pre-School Learning Alliance – which runs 110 nurseries in deprived areas – has been left with a shortfall, and individual childminders also say they have been left out of pocket because the government subsidy doesn't fully cover costs.

63 **If just 10 per cent more mothers worked, they could generate an estimated additional £1.5 billion for the UK economy:** https://www.ippr.org/files/publications/pdf/No-more-baby-steps_Jun2014.pdf?noredirect=1

63 **Universal free childcare could earn the nation up to £37 billion through higher tax revenues and lower benefit payments:** https://d3n8a8pro7vhmx.cloudfront.net/womensequality/pages/2512/attachments/original/1495027355/WE_3495_Manifesto_2017_V5_Singles.pdf?1495027355

63 **That seems to me a good way to make society more equal:** https://www.familyandchildcaretrust.org/putting-quality-heart-early-years

64 **Slovenia and Chile invests significantly more of their GDP in childcare than we do:** http://www.oecd.org/education/school/SS%20V%20Spending%20on%20early%20childhood%20education%20and%20care.png

64 **A McDonald's 'crew member' aged twenty-five or over gets that to flip burgers:** https://www.employeebenefits.co.uk/issues/january-2018/mcdonalds-recommends-pay-increase-for-115000-uk-staff/

75 **since the global financial crash of 2008 and women have accounted for much of the rise:** Women accounted for 58 per cent of the rise in the seven years to 2015, https://www.gov.uk/government/uploads/system/uploads/attachment_data/file/500317/self-employed-income.pdf

75 **They are now at the helm of one in three female-owned businesses – compared to one in six twenty years ago:** https://www.theatlantic.com/business/archive/2015/04/women-are-owning-more-and-more-small-businesses/390642/

76 **reason for starting their business was 'to have considerable freedom to adapt my approach to work':** http://www.enterpriseresearch.ac.uk/wp-content/uploads/2017/07/GEM-UK-2016_final.pdf

76 **our full potential remains untapped because women are still only about half as likely as men to be entrepreneurs:** Ibid.

76 **And, once again, there are barriers for us to overcome: from access to finance:** Female entrepreneurs in the UK are 1.7 times less likely to say they can access the money

needed to start a business, http://www.oecd.org/cfe/smes/
Policy-Brief-on-Women-s-Entrepreneurship.pdf; just 15 per
cent of the US companies that received venture capital
funding between 2011 and 2013 had women on the executive
team, http://entrepreneurship.babson.edu/changing-the-
status-quo-in-venture-capital/?_ga=2.104028992.1395481516.
1519295797-1027792271.1519295797; women are two-thirds
less likely to invest in entrepreneurs than men, http://gem-
consortium.org/report/49860

76 **the fact that we're more likely to start businesses in
lower-earning sectors:** Lower-earning sectors include health
and social work, https://www.fsb.org.uk/docs/default-source/
fsb-org-uk/fsb-women-in-enterprise-the-untapped-potential
febc2bbb4fa86562a286ffooooodc48fe.pdf?sfvrsn=0

76 **or a lack of affordable childcare:** A quarter of female
business owners surveyed by the Federation of Small
Businesses said they believed that a lack of available and
affordable childcare stopped women starting up alone,
https://www.fsb.org.uk/docs/default-source/fsb-org-uk/fsb-
women-in-enterprise-the-untapped-potentialfebc2bbb4fa8
6562a286ffooooodc48fe.pdf?sfvrsn=0

76 **That's an awful lot of money we're not seeing because
women's full potential isn't being realized:** It's estimated
that women would add £150 billion extra to the UK economy
by 2025 if more of us started our own businesses, https://
www.womensbusinesscouncil.co.uk/wpcontent/uploads/
2017/02/DfE-WBC-Two-years-on-report_update_AW_
CC.pdf

76 **Women who are self-employed earn £243 a week on
average compared to £428 in full-time employment:**
https://www.cipd.co.uk/knowledge/work/trends/mega
trends/self-employment

77 **People who work for themselves are more likely to feel satisfied than those in other employment:** https://www.cipd.co.uk/Images/more-selfies_2018-a-picture-of-self-employment-in-the-UK_tcm18-37250.pdf

98 **and a key argument is that diversity is good for the bottom line:** There is much research in this area but here are two typical examples. Companies in the top 25 per cent for gender diversity were 21 per cent more likely to have above average financial returns. Companies that had improved racial and ethnic diversity were 33 per cent more likely to outperform industry peers, https://www.mckinsey.com/business-functions/organization/our-insights/delivering-through-diversity. Businesses with more women on the board outperformed those with fewer women by up to 84 per cent on three key financial criteria, http://www.catalyst.org/knowledge/bottom-line-corporate-performance-and-womens-representation-boards-2004-2008

100 **maximize shareholder value – otherwise known as making the most money:** https://www.ft.com/content/e392f12c-adac-11e2-82b8-00144feabdc0

100 **The idea of maximizing profits took hold:** https://www.forbes.com/sites/stevedenning/2013/07/09/ft-urges-business-schools-to-stop-teaching-the-worlds-dumbest-idea/#295afd7f2554

100 **In 1989, it was fifty-nine times and in 1965 a mere twenty:** https://www.epi.org/publication/ceo-pay-remains-high-relative-to-the-pay-of-typical-workers-and-high-wage-earners/

100 **a CEO makes £129 for every pound the average employee makes. In 1987, it was £45:** https://www.cipd.co.uk/Images/7571-ceo-pay-in-the-ftse100-report-web_tcm18-26441.pdf

101 **and will make up three-quarters of the global workforce by 2025:** http://www.ey.com/Publication/vwLUAssets/EY-global-generations-a-global-study-on-work-life-challenges-across-generations/$FILE/EY-global-generations-a-global-study-on-work-life-challenges-across-generations.pdf

101 **flexible working and aversion to excessive overtime:** Ibid.

102 **Millennials place greater importance on team cohesion, supervisor support and flexibility:** Ibid.

115 **The good news is that almost half of us in the UK don't work for the big hitters:** http://smallbusiness.co.uk/smes-driving-employment-levels-2539643/

120 **core belief that the way business works should enable 'everyone to do the work they love':** https://www.workspace.co.uk/community/homework/technology/the-ai-business-disrupting-how-you-run-your-office

131 **Then the players turned up at his house, asked him to return, and he decided to do so but start again from scratch:** http://www.espn.co.uk/football/uefa-europa-league/0/blog/post/3203187/ostersunds-fk-tiny-swedish-team-believe-they-can-dominate-european-football and https://www.theguardian.com/football/copa90/2018/feb/22/ostersunds-club-sweden-arsenal-europa-league

132 **working with local refugee centres and putting on a stage show of *Swan Lake*:** http://www.espn.co.uk/football/uefa-europa-league/0/blog/post/3203187/ostersunds-fk-tiny-swedish-team-believe-they-can-dominate-european-football

134 **almost half of straight white men do so too:** https://www2.deloitte.com/content/dam/Deloitte/us/Documents/about-deloitte/us-inclusion-uncovering-talent-paper.pdf

136   appraisal and get that [grade] four [. . .], which means that they stay where they are: https://live.ft.com/Events/2017/FT-Women-At-The-Top?=&v=5602645847001

139   Ulukaya decided he wanted to make a difference: https://nrf.com/blog/the-chobani-way-insights-build-culture-and-community

139   employees got full healthcare and were paid above the minimum wage: https://www.huffingtonpost.co.uk/entry/chobani-ceo-refugee-immigrant-hamdi-ulukaya_us_58189ac4e4b0990edc336cab

139   worth more than $1 million to the longest-standing workers, when it is floated or sold: https://www.nytimes.com/2016/04/27/business/a-windfall-for-chobani-employees-stakes-in-the-company.html

139   Today 10 per cent of Chobani's profits go to charity: https://givingpledge.org/Pledger.aspx?id=304

139   to challenge what Ulukaya believes is a broken system of mass food production: https://chobaniincubator.com/about/

139   Some 30 per cent of Chobani workers are refugees: https://www.youtube.com/watch?v=dApJnaaNwQY

139   Ulukaya has pledged to give the majority of his personal wealth to humanitarian causes: https://givingpledge.org/Pledger.aspx?id=304

139   Its aim is to aid twenty million dispossessed men, women and children: https://www.tent.org/about/

140   World Economic Forum in 2016. 'We can do what entrepreneurs do best: hack the way we handle this problem': http://money.cnn.com/2016/01/20/news/refugees-business-davos-opinion/

140 Ulukaya has been attacked by the far right and received death threats: https://www.fastcompany.com/3068681/how-chobani-founder-hamdi-ulukaya-is-winning-americas-culture-war

140 'from my experience [that] the minute the refugee has a job, that's the minute they stop being a refugee': https://www.youtube.com/watch?v=dApJnaaNwQY

144 'the only way we could be more professionally equal is if we were the same person,' wrote Hadley Freeman: https://www.theguardian.com/lifeandstyle/2018/mar/03/spot-working-mother-happy-busy-caretaker

145 'and have a much broader concept about what a good man is': https://www.theatlantic.com/video/index/400160/women-and-work/

146 Some 7.3 million British workers are now working flexibly: https://www.ons.gov.uk/employmentandlabourmarket/peopleinwork/earningsandworkinghours/adhocs/005248peopleinemploymentwithaflexibleworkingpatternbygender

146 just 12 per cent of positions with salaries over £20,000 are advertised as such: http://timewise.co.uk/wp-content/uploads/ 2017/06/Timewise-Flexible-Jobs-Index-2017.pdf

148 offer time and help to nurseries in exchange for fee reductions of up to 50 per cent, is well established: https://b.3cdn.net/nefoundation/c142e402b391ed2097_z7m6ibzpa.pdf

148 offset by increased taxes, National Insurance and VAT payments, as well as a reduced benefits bill: https://www.theguardian.com/commentisfree/2018/may/23/britain-productivity-crisis-meghan-duchess-female-empowerment

148 then scale up to a maximum of £4 per hour for those with a salary of more than £66,000: https://www.family andchildcaretrust.org/creating-anti-poverty-childcare-system

149 91 per cent of the costs are recouped through tax breaks, employee retention and employee engagement: https:// www.fastcompany.com/3062792/patagonias-ceo-explains- how-to-make-onsite-child-care-pay-for-itself

149 The company also has around a fifty:fifty gender split in management: https://work.qz.com/806516/the-secret-to- patagonias-success-keeping-moms-and-onsite-child-care- and-paid-parental-leave/

151 which has health and emotional benefits for them and their children: https://www.oecd.org/policy-briefs/ parental-leave-where-are-the-fathers.pdf

152 around 3 per cent of working fathers have taken it: https://www.ft.com/content/2c4e539c-9a0d-11e7-a652-cde3f 882dd7b

152 About half of the fathers surveyed in 2017 said they would take SPL: http://www.workingfamilies.org.uk/ news/half-of-fathers-would-use-shared-parental-leave-survey- finds/

152 report that they have been sacked after asking about family-friendly policies: http://www.parliament.uk/ business/committees/committees-a-z/commons-select/ women-and-equalities-committee/news-parliament-2015/ fathers-workplace-evidence1-16-17/

152 could take up to a year of leave on full pay after the birth or adoption of a child: https://media.netflix.com/en/ company-blog/starting-now-at-netflix-unlimited-maternity- and-paternity-leave

152 **Aviva now offers twenty-six weeks' leave on full basic pay to its employees:** https://www.aviva.com/newsroom/news-releases/2017/11/Aviva-announces-equal-paid-parental-leave/

152 **would earn less than their female partners have been upheld by employment tribunals:** https://pjhlaw.co.uk/employment-tribunal-procedure/enhanced-paternity-pay

153 **government to look at introducing ring-fenced leave for fathers as an alternative to shared parental leave:** https://www.parliament.uk/business/committees/committees-a-z/commons-select/women-and-equalities-committee/news-parliament-2017/fathers-and-the-workplace-report-17-19/

153 **Iceland and Germany, where the financial offer is much more robust:** When the Swedish government introduced a 'use it or lose it' policy, the introduction of the 'daddy month' saw take-up shoot up from under 10 per cent to almost half of fathers, http://www.tavinstitute.org/news/shared-parental-leave-minimal-impact-gender-equality/

In 2000, Icelandic fathers and mothers were both given three months' parental leave – at 80 per cent of their average salary – and a further three months to share between them. In 2017, nearly three-quarters of Icelandic fathers took time off, https://grapevine.is/news/2017/04/06/fewer-men-taking-paternity-leave/

When the Germans introduced two paid bonus months, the number of fathers taking leave increased by 50 per cent. Within six years of the policy being introduced, a third of German dads were taking time off, http://oecdinsights.org/2016/03/08/international-womens-day-what-fathers-can-do-for-gender-equality/

153 **Just 2 per cent of fathers took advantage of the leave available in 2015:** https://qz.com/928022/japan-leads-the-

world-in-paid-paternity-but-fails-on-nearly-every-other-measure-of-workplace-gender-equality/

154   **regularly overworking causes a significantly increased risk of everything from strokes to diabetes:** https://www.tuc.org.uk/international-issues/europe/workplace-issues/work-life-balance/15-cent-increase-people-working-more

154   **'Oh, you're off early again':** https://publications.parliament.uk/pa/cm201719/cmselect/cmwomeq/358/358.pdf

160   **Corner shops ran out of sausages as dads rushed to find something easy to cook for tea:** http://www.bbc.co.uk/news/magazine-34602822

160   **'It completely paralysed the country and opened the eyes of many men':** Ibid.

161   **she posted a simple message on the Facebook page of a political group: 'I think we should march':** https://www.reuters.com/article/us-usa-trump-women/hawaii-grandmas-plea-launches-womens-march-in-washington-idUSKBN13U0GW

163   **the crisis of extreme masculinity, which is this sort of behaviour:** https://www.youtube.com/watch?v=jT-oTrovgCo

163   **sexual harassment at work and the most common perpetrators were senior colleagues:** https://www.equalityhumanrights.com/sites/default/files/ending-sexual-harassment-at-work.pdf

163   **'a lack of consistent, effective action on the part of too many employers':** Ibid.

164   **those under twenty-eight, and women directors or board members:** https://gender.bitc.org.uk/system/files/research/project_28-40_the_report.pdf

164 **including the ability to feed our families and preserve our reputations:** http://time.com/5018813/farmworkers-solidarity-hollywood-sexual-assault/

166 **Barely one in ten UK women earn equal to or more on average than their male colleagues:** Just 11.2 per cent of UK women earn equal or more on average than their male colleagues, https://ig.ft.com/gender-pay-gap-UK/

166 **'I felt a sap,' she wrote. 'For years I had been subsidizing other people's lifestyles':** https://www.thetimes.co.uk/article/sarah-montague-on-her-gender-pay-gap-im-furious-about-being-paid-less-than-men-at-the-bbc-t9vkfjqko

FURTHER READING

Some Essential Readings on Gender and Feminism

Friedan, Betty, *The Feminine Mystique* (Penguin, Harmondsworth, 1965)

De Beauvoir, Simone, *The Second Sex* (Vintage Books, New York, 1989)

hooks, bell, *Ain't I a Woman: Black Women and Feminism* (Pluto, London, 1982)

Lerner, Gerda, *The Creation of Patriarchy* (Oxford University Press, USA, 1986)

Millett, Kate, *Sexual Politics* (Virago, London, 1977)

Oakley, Ann, *Sex, Gender and Society* (Maurice Temple Smith, London, 1972)

Scott, Joan Wallach, 'Gender as a useful category of historical analysis', in *Culture, Society and Sexuality*, pp. 77–97(Routledge, London, 2006)

Segal, Lynne, *Is The Future Female? Troubled Thoughts on Contemporary Feminism* (Virago, London, 1987)

Contemporary Feminist Readings (post 1990s) and Critiques

Adichie, Chimamanda Ngozi, *We Should all be Feminists* (Vintage, London, 2014)

Beard, Mary, *Women and Power: A Manifesto* (Profile Books, London, 2017)

Collins, Patricia Hill, *Black Feminist Thought: Knowledge, Consciousness, and the Politics of Empowerment* (Routledge, New York, 1991)

Faludi, Susan, *Stiffed: The Betrayal of Modern Man* (Vintage, London, 2000)

Gay, Roxane, *Bad Feminist* (Harper Collins, New York, 2014)

Moran, Caitlin, *How to Be a Woman* (Ebury, London, 2011)

Rottenberg, Catherine, *The Rise of Neoliberal Feminism* (Oxford University Press, Oxford, 2018)

Wolf, Naomi, *The Beauty Myth* (Vintage, New York, 1991)

Young, Iris Marion, *On Female Body Experience: 'Throwing Like a Girl' and Other Essays* (Cambridge University Press, Cambridge, 2005)

Women, Men and Gender at Work

Barber, Elizabeth Wayland, *Women's Work: The First 20,000 Years: Women, Cloth, and Society in Early Times* (WW Norton & Company, London, 1995)

Cockburn, Cynthia K., *In the Way of Women: Men's Resistance to Sex Equality in Organizations* (Macmillan, London, 1991)

Davidson, Marilyn J., and Cooper, Cary L., *Shattering the Glass Ceiling: The Woman Manager* (Paul Chapman Publishing, London, 1992)

Gregory, Abigail and Milner, Susan, 'Work–Life Balance: A Matter of Choice?', in *Gender, Work & Organization* (16, 1 (2009): 1–13)

Hearn, Jeff, and Parkin, Wendy, *Sex at Work: The Power and Paradox of Organisation Sexuality* (Macmillan, London, 1987)

Martin, Joanne, 'Deconstructing organizational taboos: The suppression of gender conflict in organizations', in *Organization Science* (1, 4 (1990): 339–359)

Roper, Michael, *Masculinity and the British Organization Man since 1945* (Oxford University Press, Oxford, 1994)

Simpson, Ruth and Lewis, Patricia, *Voice, Visibility and the Gendering of Organizations* (Palgrave Macmillian, London, 2007)

Do We Want to Be Leaders?

Ashcraft, Karen Lee, 'The Glass Slipper: "Incorporating" Occupational Identity in Management Studies', *Academy of Management Review* (38, 1 (2013): 6–31)

Collinson, David, and Hearn, Jeff (Eds), *Men as Managers, Managers as Men: Critical*

Perspectives on Men, Masculinities and Managements (Sage, London, 1996)

Kelan, Elisabeth, *Rising Stars: Developing Millennial Women as Leaders* (Palgrave Macmillan, London, 2012)

Nelson, Julie, *Gender and Risk-Taking: Economics, Evidence, and Why the Answer Matters* (Routledge, London, 2017)

Saini, Angela, *Inferior: How Science Got Women Wrong – and the New Research that's Rewriting the Story* (Fourth Estate, London, 2017)

Oakley, Judith G., 'Gender-based barriers to senior management positions: Understanding the scarcity of female CEOs', *Journal of Business Ethics* (27, 4 (2000): 321–334)

The Elephant in the Room – Gender, Work and the Family

Folbre, Nancy, *Who Pays for the Kids?* (Routledge, London, 1994)

Hochschild, Arlie, and Machung, Anne, *The Second Shift: Working Families and the Revolution at Home* (Penguin, London, 2012)

Slaughter, Anne-Marie, *Unfinished Business: Women Men Work Family* (Oneworld, London, 2015)

Tilly, Louise, and Scott, Joan Wallach, *Women, Work, and Family* (Psychology Press, Hove, 1989)

Williams, Joan, *Unbending Gender: Why Family and Work Conflict and What to do about it* (Oxford University Press, Oxford, 2001)

Gender and Transformation

Cho, Sumi, and Williams Crenshaw, Kimberlé, and McCall, Leslie, 'Toward a Field of Intersectionality Studies: Theory, Applications, and Praxis', in *Signs: Journal of Women in Culture and Society* (38, 4 (2013): 785–810)

Connell, Raewyn W., 'Change among the Gatekeepers: Men, Masculinities, and Gender Equality in the Global Arena', in *Signs: Journal of Women in Culture and Society* (30, 3 (2005): 1801–1825)

Fraser, Nancy, 'Feminist Politics in the Age of Recognition: A two-dimensional Approach to Gender Justice', in *Studies in Social Justice* (1, 1 (2007): 23–35)

Kabeer, Naila, *Paid Work, Women's Empowerment and Gender Justice: Critical Pathways of Social Change,* Pathways of Empowerment working papers, 3 (Institute of Development Studies, Brighton, 2008)

Winker, Gabriele, and Degele, Nina, 'Intersectionality as multi-level analysis: Dealing with social inequality', in *European Journal of Women's Studies* (18, 1 (2011): 51–66)

ACKNOWLEDGEMENTS

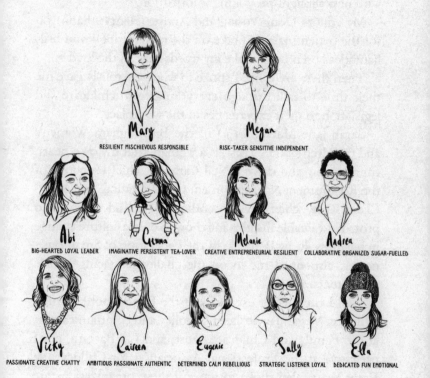

Mary
RESILIENT MISCHIEVOUS RESPONSIBLE

Megan
RISK-TAKER SENSITIVE INDEPENDENT

Abi
BIG-HEARTED LOYAL LEADER

Gemma
IMAGINATIVE PERSISTENT TEA-LOVER

Melanie
CREATIVE ENTREPRENEURIAL RESILIENT

Andrea
COLLABORATIVE ORGANIZED SUGAR-FUELLED

Vicky
PASSIONATE CREATIVE CHATTY

Caireen
AMBITIOUS PASSIONATE AUTHENTIC

Eugenie
DETERMINED CALM REBELLIOUS

Sally
STRATEGIC LISTENER LOYAL

Ella
DEDICATED FUN EMOTIONAL

A book, like a film or a magazine, is all about lots of people coming together to create something. So while I'm the voice of this story, there are many people to thank for helping to bring *Work Like a Woman* to life.

First up, my co-writer Megan Lloyd Davies. My trust in her talent enabled me to fly.

Dr Wendy Hein, lecturer in marketing at Birkbeck College, whose research expertise in gender, marketing and organizations helped make sense of facts and provided me with new thought-provoking information.

My editors Doug Young and Andrea Henry: thank you for the patient, talented take on the manuscript – and brilliant ideas on how to make my words sing all the louder.

Then there are those I spoke to who generously gave me their time to talk through everything from childcare and legislation to their experiences in the workplace.

Sarah-Jane Marsh, CEO of the Birmingham Women's and Children's NHS Trust, is a woman after my own heart: funny, gutsy and driven. Neil Carberry, chief executive of the Recruitment & Employment Confederation, and Mary-Clare Race, chief creative officer of Mind Gym, also provided valuable insights into how to create culture change in business. Ruby Peacock, of the Federation of Small Businesses, also filled me in on the challenges facing female entrepreneurs.

Neil Leitch, chief executive of the Pre-School Learning Alliance, Megan Jarvie, head of policy and communications at the Family and Childcare Trust, and Liz Bayram, chief executive at the Professional Association for Childcare & Early Years, also spoke to me. All these organizations are doing critical work to both provide and improve the childcare available to us all – and campaign to make things better. I salute you all.

Lisa Unwin, of She's Back, talked eloquently of the challenges facing women returning to work after taking time out to care, and I love that she's tackling this vital issue so passionately – and practically.

Nelly Murenzi is a bright, fabulous woman who spoke to me so intelligently about the challenges she's faced that I was tempted to try and persuade her to switch careers for one in retail. Kate Nowlan, chief executive of CiC, told me about the award-winning work she's done to make work flexible for her employees. Good on you, Kate.

Leon Barron, a senior lecturer in forensic science at King's College London, spoke to me about combining care with being a father. We need more men like you.

Peter Godsell, who looks after HR for Ford in Europe, the Middle East and Africa, and Kevin Clarkson, who runs the Ford Parents Network, also spoke to me about what they're doing in a huge business to better integrate work and family life. Thank you all for your time and insights.

And then my homies. The rock-steady crew who were always there, believing in me, but always letting me know if I was talking absolute bull.

Melanie Rickey. Caireen Wackett. Abi Sangster. Gemma Nightingale. Eugenie Furniss. Sally Wray. Vicky Palmer. Ella Horne. Women of strength, courage, kindness and a wicked sense of humour. Together we will change the world of work.

INDEX

ABOUT THE AUTHOR

Mary Portas is one of the UK's most high-profile business-women. After making her name transforming Harvey Nichols into London's sexiest fashion destination, Mary launched her own retail consultancy working for clients ranging from Louis Vuitton to Mercedes, started a career in TV, advised the government on the future of high streets, developed a fashion label and wrote two books. Her proudest achievement to date is the creation of twenty-six Mary's Living & Giving shops for Save the Children.

Today Mary's agency Portas advises retail clients from every continent, and the business's success is built on an obsessive understanding of human and cultural behaviour. This kind of empathy, along with intuition, creativity and collaboration are what drive Mary's business – as well as her quest to make work and how we consume and commune better for us all by tapping into feminine values.